# INDIAN WELLS VALLEY

## AND NORTHERN MOJAVE DESERT

# HANDBOOK

by the

China Lake–Ridgecrest Branch of the

American Association of University Women

*Seventh Edition*

ISBN: 0–9649578-1-7

Library of Congress Catalog Card Number: 2001094500

Printed by Seagull Press, Salt Lake City, Utah

Cover Photographs

Front Cover: *Indian Wells Valley* by Mark Pahuta

Back Cover: *Big Petroglyph Canyon* by Mark Pahuta

*Roadrunner*, courtesy of Historical Society of the Upper Mojave Desert

# Dedication

This edition is dedicated to the early members of our local AAUW whose perseverance, dedication, vitality, and enthusiasm helped weave the fabric of our community to make it the unique place we call home.

# Acknowledgments

Managing Editor:           Beatrice Smith

Editor:                       Elizabeth Babcock

Steering Committee:       Sandy Beaulieu, Ph.D.
Beatrice Smith

Review and Proofreading:  Miriam Cartwright, Ph.D.
Georgia Cabe
Jane Crow
Donnie Goettig
Beatrice Smith

Cover Design:             Sue Dunker

Distribution              Bonnie Jones

As with every edition of this handbook, we have built on the foundation of previous editions. Elsa Pendleton and Betty Gross, managing editors of the sixth edition, deserve special thanks for the foundation they provided for our work.

The following people assisted with the sixth and seventh editions of the handbook. We thank them for their time, energy, and interest. This is truly a community handbook.

| | |
|---|---|
| Gary Babcock | Frank Monastero, Ph.D. |
| Judy Breitenstein | Jim Nichols |
| Carroll L. Evans, Jr. | Don Moore |
| Bill Ferguson, M.D. | Mark Pahuta |
| Linn Gum | Tom Roseman |
| Anna Hearn | Hilliary Smith |
| Mary Ann Henry | Lloyd Smith, Ph.D. |
| Mary Lundstrom | Janet Westbrook |
| Gladys Merrick | Elva Younkin |

We gratefully acknowledge *The Saturday Evening Post* and the Kern County Historical Society for material quoted in Part 1. Bird drawings on pages 139-159 are from *Birds of the Pacific States*, copyright 1927 by Ralph Hoffman, renewed 1955 by Gertrude W. Hoffman. Reprinted by permission of Houghton Mifflin Co., all rights reserved.

# Contents

# Introduction

The China Lake–Ridgecrest Branch of the American Association of University Women is proud to present this seventh edition of the *Indian Wells Valley and Northern Mojave Desert Handbook*. The handbook has been serving this valley ever since we published our first edition in 1948, the same year China Lake received its own post office and was thus officially designated a community and only a year after the Inyokern–China Lake Branch of AAUW was founded.

The valley's first major population explosion had occurred with the Navy's arrival on the desert just five years earlier. This handbook has been our valley's primary guidebook through most of a recent history that saw three distinct communities — Ridgecrest, Inyokern, and China Lake — grow virtually from a sandbox. A highly educated workforce moved into this remote corner of the world and, with a "can-do" attitude, made major contributions to the defense of our country.

This important work meant that people from throughout the United States needed to leave their homes for an environment where sandstorms, desert creatures, and deficiencies in housing, shopping, and transportation all presented challenges. The newcomers met those challenges and built a community unlike any other. The camaraderie, the close friendships, the safety of a small community, and the adrenaline rush of innovation to meet the needs of national defense blended together to create an environment difficult to define.

The newcomers soon discovered and grew to relish dazzling sunsets, clear air, vistas of incredible beauty, and carpets of wildflowers in the spring. Today we continue to glory in those assets, as well as our beautiful mountains, nearly perpetual sunshine, spacious vistas, and sparkling starlit evenings. In winter we enjoy the halo of snow capping the local foothills, and after a rare rain we revel in the clean, creosote-scented air and blue sky.

As valley residents grew to love this environment, they also established clubs and social services to make life here more comfortable. At the center of that drive to meet social and community needs was our local AAUW branch. From founding the first nursery school and the Desert Counseling Clinic, to hosting local candidate nights, to setting up and administering scholarship programs, to providing bridge groups, gourmet dining groups, play-reading groups, and educational programs. AAUW has been an integral part of our community.

After our 1948 handbook met with success, we published five more editions, including an extensively revised and expanded sixth edition in 1996. When we began our revisions to that popular edition, we realized that the impact of the Desert Protection Act and other changes since the previous edition necessitated a new edition, built on the one that preceded it.

We hope this handbook gives you glimpses of our desert, our community, our natural environment, and the people who made their home in this fascinating valley.

— *The Editors*

*Former U.S.O. Club reflected in flower-shop window*      *— Mark Pahuta*

# Part One
# HISTORY OF
# INDIAN WELLS VALLEY
# AND THE NORTHERN
# MOJAVE DESERT

*Indian Wells Valley* — *Mark Pahuta*

# HISTORY

## The First People

The first people known to settle in Indian Wells Valley lived here sometime between 11,000 and 9,000 years ago. Archaeologists believe the "Paleoindian" culture was adapted to hunting the mammoth, camel, Pleistocene bison, and now-extinct American horse. Fluted points characteristic of Paleoindians have been found at sites in the vicinity of the Coso Range. Rock art had been made as early as 16,500 years before present, but these petroglyphs may have been made by outsiders.

More evidence of human habitation dates from between about 9,000 and 7,000 years ago, when western North America was cooler and wetter than it is now. Like all the valleys of the Great Basin, the Indian Wells Valley was full of water. Prehistoric China Lake skirted the southern and western sides of the Cosos.

Evidence from scattered surface sites suggests that hunting took place in the region. A few more substantial sites contained spear points, knives, scrapers, and choppers — evidence of a mobile hunting society that exploited a wide variety of game. Such sites were not found near the lakeshore; the lakes of this time were saline with shores largely unsuitable for village locations. The obsidian source at Sugarloaf Mountain, the broad obsidian dome looming to the east of U.S. 395 eight miles north of Little Lake, appears to have been first exploited during this period. Rock art continued to be made.

The period of about 7,000 to 4,000 years ago was apparently hot and dry. Temperatures rose enough to dry up the pluvial lakes and cause a change in vegetation. Grasses and succulents disappeared, while Joshua tree woodlands and

*Petroglyphs at Sheep Canyon*                    *— Mark Pahuta*

pine forests moved to higher, cooler elevations. Evidence exists that humans were present at scattered sites.

The first clear evidence of a prehistoric village near Indian Wells Valley dates from this era. In 1948-51, when members of the Southwest Museum in Los Angeles excavated the Stahl Site, a cave and surrounding area near Little Lake, they found evidence of dark, organic soils typical of later villages.

Other evidence suggests that the village was small — perhaps only 20 to 30 people at a time. Tools found at the site showed reliance on hunting and gathering. Grinding tools showed that plant foods were being used increasingly. The site also contained Pinto projectile points, relatively short, squat spear points with wide bases. Such points — the diagnostic artifacts of the period — have been found elsewhere in a wide range of environments, but the Stahl Site is still the only significant village of the period that has been found near our valley.

Between 4,000 and 1,500 years ago, the environment became somewhat wetter and cooler, similar to the conditions of today. With the less hostile environment came an expansion of human settlement. Use of the Little Lake site continued, and villages were established at other locations, with the occupants ranging over many environments and using many plant and animal foods. Mining of the obsidian at Sugarloaf Mountain intensified, with some of that obsidian used for trade. Local obsidian has been found as far away as the Los Angeles coast, while coastal trade items, especially shell beads, appeared in Coso villages.

The late prehistoric period, extending from 1,500 to 800 years ago, saw some important changes. Sometime around 500 A.D., the bow and arrow replaced the earlier atlatl (throwing board and spear). Local cultures also began using the pine nut for food, with large pine-nut gathering camps located at high elevations near piñon groves.

Around 800 to 150 years ago, the Numic or Shoshonean people appeared. With them came new styles of projectile points and, for the first time, simple brownware ceramics. The most dramatic change was the reduced use or abandonment of winter villages. Pine nuts and seeds became the prime diet staple, with meat protein less important and derived increasingly from small animals. At the same time, much less obsidian mining went on at Sugarloaf Mountain.

The Shoshoneans used Indian Wells Valley for hunting and gathering until the early 20th century, when mining, ranching, and homesteading made that earlier lifestyle impossible. Shoshonean groups in this area were the Northern Paiutes (who called themselves "Nuwii," meaning simply "people") of the Owens Valley area, the Kosos or Panamint Shoshones to the east, the Southern Paiutes (Tubatulabals, or "pine-nut eaters," who occupied the tributaries of the Kern River), and the Kawaiisu who lived near Tehachapi and used the territory to the east, including Death Valley.

The local Native American population was never large. Individuals needed to roam over great areas to eke out a living from their harsh surroundings. Major foods were pine nuts, seeds, dried grubs, cactus joints, mesquite bean pods, and other natural foods. Each settlement had a few hunters with large bows and arrows or spears who shared their kill with the whole community. Within the 19th century, the Kawaiisu still organized springtime hunting parties into what are now Navy range areas at China Lake to hunt antelope and bighorn sheep.

Our early settlers left behind many artifacts, chief among them the petroglyphs found abundantly in canyons located on the China Lake north ranges. Although some of the petroglyphs may be of Shoshonean origin, Shoshonean descendants within the last few generations have been unable to explain the meaning of these symbols. Recent studies point toward ritual or shamanic origins. The Paiutes believed the petroglyphs to have been the work of Hy-nan-nu, a legendary superman who, according to Paiute stories, roamed the area preaching and performing good deeds.

Other legends concern Black Mountain, the dark mountain on the southwest skyline of Indian Wells Valley. Members of various tribes were believed to have come from great distances to attend secret peacemaking rites on the mountain. Remains of a village, campsites, petroglyphs, caves, and artifacts have been found there.

The Maturango Museum, 100 E. Las Flores Ave., Ridgecrest, is an excellent place to learn about the petroglyphs and other aspects of the cultural and natural history of the Northern Mojave Desert. The museum is open every day from 10 a.m. to 5 p.m.

# Explorers

Many historians believe that the first white explorer to enter Indian Wells Valley was Joseph Reddeford Walker who, having heard of the pass from Indians living in the Kern

Canyon, traveled in 1834 through the valley of the Kern and eastward over the pass that now bears his name. In 1843 Walker guided the Joseph B. Chiles party, the second wagon train to enter California from the east, down from Owens Valley, where the party abandoned its wagons, and went on over Walker Pass.

In 1845 Walker led another party over the pass. After deciding that 43 of the party were unable to stand the rigors of a more northern route, government explorer John C. Frémont sent them south over Walker Pass with Walker and Theodore Talbot, while Frémont and a hardy few, including Kit Carson and Richard Owens, explored along the Truckee. On that trip, Edward Kern mapped the river that Frémont later named for him.

*Joseph Reddeford Walker*
*— Maturango Museum*

Probably the first white settlers to cross Indian Wells Valley were some of the famed Death Valley '49ers in 1849. More prudent members of the party traveled the old Spanish Trail to the south, thus avoiding much hardship. The '49ers took several routes to escape Death Valley. A group from Mississippi and Georgia toiled across the mountains to Owens Valley, then went south beside the Sierra Nevada; other groups apparently entered Indian Wells Valley via Wilson Canyon or Shepherd Canyon in the Argus Range and passed across what are now China Lake ranges toward the Sierra Nevada.

One evening in early January 1850, William Lewis Manly and John Rogers, who had set out ahead of the faltering Bennett and Arcane families to bring them aid, came upon a campfire at Indian Wells, a sparkling spring at the mouth of Indian Wells Canyon. Thinking the camp to be Indian, they crept cautiously toward the fire and to their happy surprise viewed the faces of Captain Edward Doty and his Illinois Jayhawkers, who had reached Indian Wells by a different route.

Manly's story of his adventures with the Death Valley party is a classic tale of heroism. He and Rogers finally led the Bennett and Arcane families to safety in March 1850. If the '49ers had come through this area at any time of year but midwinter, all undoubtedly would have perished.

In 1860 Dr. Darwin French and his party searched this area for the legendary Lost Gunsight Mine (a rich vein of silver said to have been found accidentally by one of the '49ers), but discovered instead the ledges of Coso. During the next year Coso Village (now on China Lake ranges) became the most

*Death Valley Sand Dunes*                              *— Dolph Amster*

populous spot in the area as miners and adventurers, lured by exaggerated claims in the newspapers, rushed to cash in on the rumored riches.

An interesting variation of the mining traffic over Walker Pass occurred in April 1861 when the California–Nevada Boundary Survey party, in need of supplies, brought three camels to serve as a pack train through Indian Wells Valley.

In the 1860s, hard winters and the encroachment of settlers into the area brought Indian raids on cattle and the destruction of property. In 1864 Army companies were brought in to establish peace and aggressively pursue the idea of creating and populating reservation lands.

During the same era, an annual springtime sheep drive began along the half-mile-wide California Sheep Trail that extends from the west end of Kern County northward to Bodie.

## Miners and Mining Camps

In the 1870s, activity at the famous Cerro Gordo mines (rich silver, zinc, and lead deposits high above Keeler in the Owens Valley) greatly increased traffic through Indian Wells Valley. By 1871, triweekly stages traveled between Owens Valley and the rapidly growing pueblo of Los Angeles. Then in 1873, Remi Nadeau organized the Cerro Gordo Freighting Company. Nadeau's teamsters traveling to and from Cerro Gordo often fed and watered their mules at the stage stations at Indian Wells and Coyote Holes. After a few months, Nadeau scheduled regular stops at the mouth of Nine-Mile Canyon and at Coyote Holes, located near the present turnoff to Walker Pass from Highway 14. By 1874, the teams were hauling 18 tons of silver a day from Cerro Gordo through Indian Wells Valley. At its peak, the freighting service operated 80 teams, each team running 14 mules and three wagons as large as narrow-gauge boxcars.

The teams traveled in pairs, with each pair of teams plodding back and forth at two miles per hour between two

*Surprise Valley Mill, Panamint City, late 1870s*
    — *Historical Society of the Upper Mojave Desert*

of the way stations. The wagons came from Owens Valley by way of Little Lake, with an alternate route from the mining camp of Darwin going south to Junction Ranch then west to Indian Wells through Mountain Springs Canyon.

Rich silver deposits discovered in the Panamint Range in 1873 led to growth rivaling that of Cerro Gordo. Nadeau expanded his activities, and in 1874, a road cutting diagonally across Indian Wells Valley to the Panamint mines was built. By November 1874, so many Los Angeles teamsters were using the Panamint road that a stream of freight wagons was raising almost continual dust past Indian Wells and across the valley toward Panamint City. Once completed, this road facilitated growth of a second mining industry — borax from Searles Lake.

During this era, Chinese workers were substantially involved in hard-rock and borax mining, as well as in construction of the roads linking these activities with the outside world. Indeed, historical tradition holds that the Chinese presence in the area is responsible for the name "China Lake," given to the dry lakebed later used for Navy testing activities

The fruits of the mining industry plus the prevailing lawlessness attracted bandits to the area. The infamous bandit Tiburcio Vasquez and his lieutenant, Cleovaro Chavez, camped near Coyote Holes at a large rock outcropping now called Robbers' Roost in honor of their visit.

On February 25, 1874, Vasquez and Chavez attacked Freeman Raymond's stage station at Coyote Holes, later named Freeman's Junction. The eight people at the station were forced to turn over their meager valuables and to lie down on the ground nearby. One man, rumored to be drunk, refused to obey orders and was shot in the leg for his obstinacy. The entire company then waited two hours for the next stage to arrive.

*Robbers' Roost*                                              *— Mark Pahuta*

When the stage pulled in, Vasquez and Chavez demanded loot from the passengers, including Mortimer Belshaw, "Silver King" of Cerro Gordo.

The bandits made small profit from the stagecoach robbery or from the two Cerro Gordo freight wagons that pulled in later. Vasquez must have been chagrined upon opening the Wells Fargo box to find that it contained only a heavy set of law books. The disgruntled bandits finally took some horses and left, turning up next with their gang at the mining camp of Coso, where they did no harm.

When Army detachments from Camp Independence attempted to capture the bandits, they fled the area for the vicinity of Los Angeles. Vasquez was later captured and was hanged in March 1875.

Chavez and the remainder of the band carried out several robberies in the early months of 1875, their targets including William Scodie's tavern in Onyx, Little Lake Station, and Searles Station. Other bandits, notably two named Lopez and Guerro, also preyed on the stage stations in this area in early 1875.

By 1878 the Panamint strike was over. With the ore depleted, the mines shut down. After Cerro Gordo ceased operation in 1879, Owens Valley freight service declined and was finally abandoned in 1881.

## The First Los Angeles Aqueduct

Indian Wells Valley was again quiet until 1909, when construction of the first Los Angeles Aqueduct began. To facilitate transport of the heavy pipe and other supplies required for aqueduct construction, the Nevada and California (later Southern Pacific) Railroad laid track north from Mojave through Indian Wells Valley and on to Lone Pine.

Inyokern, the oldest surviving community in our valley, was known first as Siding 16 on the railroad, then as Magnolia.

*Valley's first school, Leliter, 1911*                    — U.S. Navy

Just to the north, the community of Brown, originally called Siding 18, was also growing. At Siding 17, now the intersection of Brown and Leliter roads, was the small community of Leliter.

The railroad was needed to haul equipment, people, and supplies for the Los Angeles aqueduct, an engineering marvel and an ecological disaster. The search for water began because farmers and ranchers in the San Fernando Valley required a reliable water source. Entrepreneurs and local government officials, ambitious to develop both farms and cities, found an apparently limitless water supply in the Owens Valley. William Mulholland, chief engineer for construction of the aqueduct and first superintendent of the Los Angeles Municipal Water Department, was a self-taught genius who built the 233-mile-long aqueduct, then the longest in the world.

By October 1910, the railroad had been completed and the City of Los Angeles could start the job of hauling an estimated 320,000 tons of materials needed to build the aqueduct. Brown became a busy aqueduct town with a peak population of between 2,000 and 3,000. In 1909 and 1910, many prospectors stopped at Brown on their way to the Custer mines near the head of Wilson Canyon (now on Navy land). Hundreds of the prospectors also enjoyed stopping at Coso Hot Springs to drink the water and bathe in the mud.

Most aqueduct workers did not stay on the job more than two weeks at a time. The common practice was to draw pay at the end of a 10-day period, then hike down the line to the nearest "rag camp," or tent saloon. One tunnel foreman complained that he usually had "one crew drunk, one crew sobering up, and one crew working." Despite the transience of the labor force, work on the aqueduct went well. The most difficult areas of construction were the huge inverted pipes, or siphons, that would allow the water to flow down and up the steep walls of the Sierra canyons.

On February 13, 1913, Los Angeles officials diverted the Owens River to flow into the aqueduct. Ten miles south of Little Lake, the Sand Canyon Siphon sprang a huge crack and spilled water down the north side of the ravine. Workmen repaired the damage within 48 hours, then decided to test the siphon at full capacity. Water spurted up in the air and the whole canyon wall burst loose and crashed into the ravine. The concrete siphon had to be abandoned, and a steel siphon built on the surface instead. Much to Mulholland's embarrassment, that siphon failure delayed the aqueduct's ceremonial opening by several months.

When the aqueduct project was proposed and during construction, opposition from residents of the Indian Wells and Owens Valleys was scattered. Aqueduct construction brought prosperity to businesses and new settlers into the area. But in the early 1920s a prolonged drought found the aqueduct draining more water than the Owens Valley could afford to lose. The Los Angeles Water Department failed to fulfill its promise to construct storage facilities that could have salvaged some of the water. Stories of fraud, greed, and corporate espionage began to surface.

Matters reached a head by November 16, 1924, when some Owens Valley residents seized a large spillway in the Alabama

*Sand Canyon Siphon*          —*Mark Pahuta*

Hills. They raised the floodgates and allowed the water to run back into their valley. In due course the Inyo County sheriff arrived and was politely carried off and deposited far from the aqueduct. The Owens Valley group maintained control for four days and closed the gates only upon receiving formal assurance from Los Angeles negotiators that their position would be negotiated.

The following years saw occasional sabotage, but most residents became resigned to the gradual desiccation of their land. As water flowed south through the aqueduct, Owens Lake — a body of water when the aqueduct opened — became a dry lake. Dust blowing off the dry surface of the lakebed contributed to what experts called the worst particulate-matter pollution in the United States. A second aqueduct (often called the "second barrel") was completed in 1970 and contributed to the problem.

In recent years, the Environmental Protection Agency mandated a solution, and mitigation efforts have raised hopes that the dust problem may eventually be settled.

## Homesteaders and Tourists

Stage and freight activities and work on the aqueduct brought hardy families to the area who liked what they saw. Freeman Raymond, owner of the Coyote Holes Station, became the valley's first recorded homesteader in 1894 when he received a "Cash Entry" patent on 160 acres of land surrounding the station.

Next on the scene was the William Callaway, Sr., family. In about 1906, the family occupied a tent in the desert about seven and a half miles southeast of Brown. Other early homesteaders, the Henry Schuette and Vernon Carr families, established their ranches in 1909. The Schuette sons, Hank and Fred, helped their dad raise alfalfa and run large herds of cattle over the family ranch, which occupied sizeable acreage on what are now China Lake ranges.

With increasing brine-mining operations in nearby Searles Valley came a larger demand for produce and dairy products. As a result, in 1912 a family named Robertson began farming about 440 acres surrounding what is now downtown Ridgecrest. In 1913, the Grant Bowman family homesteaded 160 acres and named their ranch "Las Flores."

*Mailtruck, Skidoo-Mojave run, 1917*              *— Historical Society*
*of the Upper Mojave Desert*

These and other early settlers gained claim to their land through provisions of several land-entry acts designed to open Western land to development and requiring only that the homesteaded land be "cleared and planted," not that anything be produced from the planting. Nevertheless, fruit trees, alfalfa, and several other crops were planted and did well; today alfalfa and pistachio trees are still grown near Inyokern.

Early in the 20th century, the growth of automobile travel and the creation of a statewide system of paved highways, including Highways 6 (now California 14) and 395, brought the first waves of true tourists to the high desert.

As the Indian Wells Valley gained inhabitants, Inyokern grew beyond its neighbors Leliter and Brown. By 1919, Inyokern had 350 registered voters. The little community had picnics, singing bees, and even a women's literary group. From 1921 to 1942, Inyokern had the valley's only telephone.

One of the town's best-known buildings was the "Hotel Believe It Or Not." Originally built as a garage, the building was pressed into service when a previous Inyokern hotel burned down in 1937.

*Hotel Believe It Or Not*

*– U.S. Navy*

After the conclusion of aqueduct construction, the community of Brown had begun a slow decline. Gradually buildings were sold, some to be used elsewhere and some to provide lumber for other purposes. Brown retained its one-room school until 1951; the school's beloved last teacher, Mrs. Ethel Mary "Tiny" Standard, taught there for 30 years.

As early as the late 1920s, air service arrived in the valley. Inyokern pioneer Clarence Ives built a private airport with two graded dirt strips and a taxiway south of California 178 and slightly to the east of the present airport. Then in the mid-1930s Trans-Sierra Flights (later TWA) received permission to fly a route from Fresno to Phoenix. As a result, the Works Progress Administration paved an emergency landing strip in Inyokern — the origin of today's Inyokern Airport. When Kern County established the first county airport system in the United States, the little airfield was officially designated Kern County Airport No. 8. During the early years of World War II, the Army Air Corps used the airport as an auxiliary field.

As Inyokern grew and Brown shrunk, another community took root across the valley. John McNeil and his wife, store owners at Inyokern, bought the Robertson ranch after its owner's death and started a dairy in 1924 near what is now the southern city limits of Ridgecrest.

Then in 1933 Robert and Jim Crum and their cousin Wilbur bought the dairy from McNeil and opened the Crum Brothers Dairy Farm, thus inspiring the name of "Crumville" for the little settlement. In 1936 Joe Fox bought the Crum property. He had come to the valley to set up and operate a diesel pump for irrigating the Bowman ranch. Fox had to dig his first well by hand through more than 60 feet of sand and caliche. His determination and labor brought him success; soon he had a flourishing alfalfa field and more than 7,000 chickens.

In 1939, Bill Bentham established a store and gas station at the intersection of Ridgecrest and China Lake boulevards, where the Bank of America now stands. The settlement's first librarian was 10-year-old Donna Bentham, paid by the county for tending a collection of books in her father's store.

Donker's Sunshine Dairy opened in 1941 near the corner of Bowman Road and Gateway Boulevard. Owner Dick

*Bentham's Corner, Ridgecrest*                    *— U.S. Navy*

Donker had established the first dairy 10 years earlier near Red Mountain .

The dairy served a huge area, with the deliveryman, Donker's son Don, driving more than a thousand miles a week. His 17-hour workday would start at 1:30 a.m., with his route extending as far as a Civilian Conservation Corps camp in Death Valley.

In 1941 Bentham decided to open the community's first post office in his store. Local citizens wanted to call the town Sierra View, but the Post Office Department notified them that California already had many "Sierras." Bentham held an election in his store to determine the official name. After the voters rejected such descriptive possibilities as Rattlesnake Gulch and Gilmore (for the brand of gas sold at Bentham's station), the name Ridgecrest won by one vote. Bentham then became Ridgecrest's first postmaster.

By 1943, Ridgecrest had grown to 15 homes and 96 residents. The Indian Wells Valley was still a quiet place, populated by homesteaders, farmers, prospectors, and ranchers. Then the Navy arrived — and the quiet days were over.

## The Navy on the Desert

Shortly after the United States entered World War II, naval strategists realized that airborne weaponry would be essential to conduct the war. The California Institute of Technology (Caltech), in Pasadena, California, began working under the sponsorship of the U.S. Office of Scientific Research to design and develop rockets that were urgently needed at the front. To test the new weapons, the Navy needed to find a large land area with clear air, many days of optimal flying conditions, and an isolated location.

After an exhaustive search of the California desert, a Navy and Caltech team enthusiastically settled on the Indian Wells

*Test squadron at Harvey Field, 1945*      *— U.S. Navy*

Valley — a sparsely populated expanse of desert running roughly 40 miles north to south and 25 miles east to west. The little airstrip at Inyokern was a decisive factor in the choice.

Under the provisions of the War Powers Act, the Navy closed down about a thousand mining and homesteading claims in the area. The Naval Ordnance Test Station (NOTS) officially came into being on Nov. 8, 1943. Harvey Field (now Inyokern Airport) was NOTS' first headquarters.

The military's arrival brought a burst of energy to Inyokern and the surrounding areas. Construction workers arrived in droves. In a remarkably short time, a huge research, development, test, and evaluation facility, including living quarters for employees and their families, began to rise on the desert near Ridgecrest.

In the meantime, a team of scientists and military men tested rockets on the bare desert, crouching behind creosote bushes to view the results.

An article in the June 29, 1946, issue of the *Saturday Evening Post*, entitled "The Navy's Land of Oz," painted this colorful picture of the secret city springing to life in the Mojave Desert:

There were only twenty-six private holdings in the huge area forty-two miles long, twenty-six miles across —1,025 square miles in all. Most of the residents were squatters, old-timers who had spent their lives on the baking desert sand. When the Navy undertook to move them off ... the shooting was with dollars. One old-timer demanded $2,500,000 for his holdings, but finally settled for $150 cash and a case of liquor. Another octogenarian, pointing to his sixth wife, who had recently given birth to a baby, contended that the waters from the spring by his house sustained his vigor; some had secret gold mines worth fantastic sums. Some of the inhabitants settled for cash and jobs. Others had to be ejected and their claims settled in court..

China Lake Village, headquarters of NOTS took shape; first a collection of Quonsets, then a Buck Rogers city of steam-heated, air-conditioned, concrete office buildings, homes, stores, theaters, gymnasium and swimming pool, bank, a 100-bed hospital, a school for 1,000 pupils, a BOQ for men, another, the WOQ, for 200 Waves, and a Scientists-Officers Club. The Navy had come to the desert to stay. What started as a $5,000,000 naval project had grown to an $85,000,000 naval base by V-J Day, and there were still labs and shops to be completed.

"We've got everything that Palm Springs has, except the reputation," said Commander John O. Richmond, the exec. "But we soon discovered that if we were going to keep people out in the desert, we had to provide them with some comforts. We hired twenty-four thousand civilians in one eight-month period of construction, yet never had more than seven thousand on the job. That's how bad the turnover was. But if they'll only stay until the desert gets them, they like it out here."

Living conditions were primitive for the first residents. Before family homes were built, husbands and wives often had to live in separate dormitories. Many workers commuted from Kernville, Little Lake, and Dunmovin (approximately 10 miles north of Little Lake on Highway 395).

The Navy provided furniture for the new houses at China Lake. A truck would roll down the street with a load of carpets or chairs, and each housewife would have her pick of the truck's contents. When someone moved away, the neighbors made haste to claim the best furniture.

The only school in the valley was an elementary school in Inyokern. School buses carried high-school students to Trona. Shopping facilities were meager, with the Navy Exchange and Commissary the primary stores for military and civilians alike.

During the late days of World War II, China Lake employees worked 12 days in a row, then had two days off. On those days there was a mass exodus to the larger cities to buy supplies.

Spirits were high in China Lake, with the military and civilian experts who arrived here to help in the defense of the nation working around the clock if needed to meet project milestones. Each success — and there were many — rated a fabulous China Lake party.

Adding to the camaraderie was the small-town lifestyle. Life in the desert was an adventure, with friendliness and a pioneering spirit making up for any deficiencies in creature comforts.

*NOTS front gate, 1956*        *— U.S. Navy*

Outside the NOTS fence, the community of Ridgecrest was also growing. In 1944, Dr. Thomas Drummond opened the Ridgecrest Hospital. Leaving the eight-bed hospital he had been running in Randsburg, he recognized the opportunities presented by a growing civilian population at China Lake. He used his own savings to build an 18-bed building, with quarters for himself and his family on the top floor.

Joe Fox generously responded to the arrival of the Navy by deeding land to Ridgecrest for churches, the Veterans of Foreign Wars building, and the historic U.S.O. Club building (later used for county offices) that still stands on West Ridgecrest Boulevard. The club, officially entitled the Federal Recreation Building, opened in 1945 for its first function — a well-attended dance and open house.

Although many of the Caltech scientists returned home with the end of World War II, others stayed — and new people arrived, motivated by the responsibility and technical challenge NOTS gave them early in their careers.

Ridgecrest commerce developed swiftly, while the town's population grew more slowly. Many China Lakers wanted to own homes, but for the first decade of the Navy's presence in the valley, the Federal Housing Authority refused to make FHA loans for home construction in an isolated area where the single employer might decamp at any time. Not until the mid-1950s did the FHA acknowledge that China Lake was a permanent

*Ridgecrest housing, 1948*                                    *— U.S. Navy*

*Drag racing at Inyokern Airport, 1959*     *— Historical Society of the Upper Mojave Desert*

base and authorize guaranteed loans for housing in the Indian Wells Valley. After that, civilian families gradually began to move from China Lake to other parts of the valley. (Widely available FHA financing did not arrive until the early 1970s.)

Until the 1950s, Ridgecrest also had its own airfield, owned by Bill Davis, who ran the Davis Flying School and sightseeing business. Inyokern's airport, Harvey Field, which had been the Navy's original air facility in the valley, was returned to Kern County in 1947. Commercial airline service connecting the field with the Lockheed Air Terminal at Burbank began on Feb. 26, 1951, with California Central Airlines' first flight of the 30-passenger DC-3, "City of Inyokern."

Then in 1954 the Dust Devils Drag Racing Club began using a taxiway north of the terminal building for races — thus starting what is now the oldest continuously used drag strip in the United States. Today Inyokern Airport not only provides a vital link to the outside world but also continues the drag-racing tradition, hosts frequent film and television productions, and welcomes many of the world's best glider pilots, who appreciate the Inyokern area for its outstanding thermal conditions.

One of the most famous of China Lake's products is the Sidewinder air-to-air missile — invented, developed, and tested in local indoor and outdoor laboratories — the world's foremost dogfight missile since 1956. The Shrike anti-radar missile, Walleye TV-guided weapon, Snakeye fin-retarded bomb, Zuni and Mighty Mouse rockets, Rockeye II cluster weapon, key concepts for the Polaris missile, and avionics hardware and software for fighter and attack aircraft are other notable concepts designed, developed, and tested right here on the Mojave Desert.

In 1967 NOTS became the Naval Weapons Center (NWC). In 1992 the name was changed again; the base and military complement were designated the Naval Air Weapons Station (NAWS), with the laboratory and associated civilian activities

*Sidewinder missile aboard U.S.S. Hancock, 1967*     — *U.S. Navy*

*Ridgecrest Civic Complex*                     *— Ray Arthur*

known as the Naval Air Warfare Center Weapons Division (NAWCWD). More changes are on the horizon. Through all those changes, China Lake people, laboratories, and test ranges have continued their contributions to the nation's defense.

The U.S. Naval Museum of Armament and Technology offers an overview of these contributions, with displays illustrating the Navy's nearly 60-year history here. Call the museum at (760) 939-3530 for information on how to obtain an access pass.

Today, as the close working relationship with the Navy continues, the Indian Wells Valley is also expanding beyond a one-industry economy. Among the promising ventures are small high-tech businesses that capitalize on a highly educated technical population, film and video location shooting, and facilities to attract retirees to the area.

*Cerro Gordo*                                                    *— John Dunk*

# OLD TOWNS WITH A COLORFUL PAST

Local history is rich with tales of explorers, miners, speculators, and scamps. As you maneuver your car up washboard roads to visit some of the old towns, you can begin to imagine the early settlers' struggle just to survive. But they also enjoyed good companionship and family life, especially during the boom years when rich mineral deposits offered opportunities to realize dreams of wealth.

This section is designed to introduce you to some of the old towns, many of them uninhabited and in an advanced state of decay, that can be reached within a day's drive from our valley. As you become familiar with the ghost towns and their surroundings, you may wish to extend your explorations to the canyons and hillsides that also attracted prospectors and ranchers.

A little knowledge of the colorful history of the old towns can greatly enhance your adventure. The Maturango Museum is a good place to find a variety of local history books. Also available are rockhounding guidebooks — small, often privately published brochures that list minerals and gemstones found in areas not rich enough to be commercially mined. Attending gem and mineral shows or participating in rockhounding expeditions will introduce you to some fascinating people, as well as to the hidden surprises they have unearthed.

Most ghost towns have suffered extensive damage from the elements, but much more damage from thoughtless — and illegal — acts by thoughtless people. (Existing legislation imposes stiff fines on those who take historical artifacts from public lands.)

So that others may enjoy the same things you enjoy, please follow the advice to take only pictures — leave only footprints. Insist that others around you do the same.

On a hot day, a cool mine shaft is most inviting, but please resist the temptation. Exploration of mine shafts is dangerous! Not only might you disturb poisonous spiders and snakes in a mine shaft, but you might also encounter other ominous possibilities — rotted timbers, lack of oxygen, and trapped carbon monoxide.

## The Rand Mining District

The colorful Rand Mining District includes a cluster of communities. The district is about 25 miles south of Ridgecrest on U.S. 395. The area, named for the rich Rand mines of South Africa, looks much as it did at the turn of the century.

Still populated are Johannesburg, a stage and railroad stopover; Randsburg, originally called Rand Camp; Atolia, site of extensive tungsten mining; and Red Mountain, born in 1919 with a rich silver strike and first called Osdick after the owners of the nearby stamp mill. Garlock is privately owned, with some historic buildings still visible from the highway. Sites such as Goler, Goler Heights, and Goler Gulch still contain active claims, but retain little evidence of their former glory days.

In 1895, gold was discovered at the site of the Yellow Aster Mine, resulting in the boom towns of Randsburg and Johannesburg. (The Yellow Aster is said to be named after a novel, *The Yellow Aster,* that the owner was reading at the time of the first strike.) During the 47 years of the mine's initial operation, the operators realized $16 million of profit.

During World War I, Atolia became a center for the mining of a rich tungsten ore, scheelite. In 1919 horn silver was discovered on Red Mountain, leading to the development of the fabulous Kelly Mine. Twenty years after the discovery of gold, more than a hundred mines were operating in the area.

Since 1984, the Rand Mining Company, a subsidiary of Glamis Gold, Inc., has operated a large open-pit mining operation just up the hill from Randsburg.

*Santa Barbara Church, Randsburg* — *Mark Pahuta*

A summer afternoon visit to Randsburg, when the desert grasses have turned to straw and even the reptiles stay in their burrows, brings a vivid appreciation of the endurance and obstinacy required to work a desert claim. The town is an excellent spot for the beginning ghost town explorer, because it has never quite lost its population, which rises and falls depending upon the fortunes of local mining activities. The

*Butte Avenue, Randsburg*                              *– Dolph Amster*

scattering of buildings on Butte Avenue, Randsburg's main street, illustrates a variety of building styles, with many of the houses featuring wide covered porches to protect residents from the sun. A collection of enterprises captures the weekend tourist's interest. One of the favorite destinations along Butte Avenue is the Randsburg General Store, with its amazing soda fountain. The fountain, shipped around Cape Horn from Boston to Pasadena, reached Randsburg in 1904.

Also worth a visit is the Randsburg Museum, open most weekends from 10 a.m. to 4 p.m. Memories of the district's glory days crowd the museum's walls and display cases.

Garlock may be reached by turning west from U.S. 395 onto the Red Rock–Randsburg Road four miles north of Johannesburg, then traveling a route roughly parallel to the Garlock Fault for eight miles. In its heyday, the town served as the Rand District's main center for water and supplies; as many as four stages a day stopped at Garlock in the 1890s.

Of interest in the nearly deserted ghost town are an old bark school building, an arrastre (a crude rock mill used to extract gold from ore), and several foundations scattered in the brush. The building just to the south of the road was once a saloon and bawdyhouse that attracted miners from all over the region.

## Near Barstow

Another way to experience the flavor of California's silver bonanza is to visit Calico Ghost Town, 10 miles northeast of Barstow. Take the Ghost Town Road exit from Interstate 15. During its glory days, the Calico Mining District produced many millions of dollars worth of silver, borax, and gold. The town lived from 1881-1907, when miners flocked to one of the state's richest silver strikes.

Later, Walter Knott of Knott's Berry Farm fame owned and preserved Calico. In 1966, he donated the town to the County of San Bernardino, which now runs the site as a 480-acre regional park.

About a third of Calico consists of the original structures, lovingly restored. The rest has been reconstructed to recreate the spirit of the Old West. For campground reservations or to learn more about the town, call 1-800-TO-CALICO.

## Searles Valley

The community of Trona, about 25 miles east of Ridgecrest on Trona Road, is a surprising mining town in that its riches are hidden beneath the vast white expanses of 12-square-mile Searles Lake.

Mining began after John and Dennis Searles, prospecting for gold in the area in 1862, collected borax crystals from the barren desert floor. John Searles opened the San Bernardino Borax and Mining Company in 1873 and began producing as much as 100 tons of borax a month. Then in 1895 Searles sold out to Francis Marion "Borax" Smith, whose Pacific Coast Borax Company made the 20-mule team a household word across the country.

Over the years, several other companies ran the mines, which are still in operation today. Millions of dollars worth of borax, potash, soda ash, tungsten, lithium, bromine, and other rarer minerals have been recovered. Trona is named for the mineral trona, used in the manufacture of baking powder, soaps, glass, and cleaning solvents.

To learn more about the area's fascinating history, visit the Old Guest House Museum and its History House, both operated by the Searles Valley Historical Society. The museum, built in around 1912 and located at 1319 Main Street, is chock-full of information about Searles Valley from its earliest mining days to today. Usual hours are Saturday from 11 a.m. to 1 p.m. and Monday and Wednesday from 9 a.m. to noon.

The History House, 83001 Panamint Street, was built as a company house in 1916 and features a wide overhanging roof

*Ballarat*                                                    *– Mark Pahuta*

to protect its occupants from the desert sun. Today the house is fully furnished down to kitchen utensils. An old "Trona Railway" caboose and a 1924 Stutz fire engine are parked in the side yard. The house is open only by arrangement with the museum, but you can see the outdoor displays any time.

## Panamint Valley

Ever since the gold-rush era, Panamint Valley has attracted miners and adventurers, with nearly every trail and road leading to historic mines and camps. Prominent among the valley's former settlements is Ballarat, once an important supply and entertainment center for miners, particularly those at Panamint City.

Go north from Trona for about 20 miles to a well-marked sign pointing toward Ballarat, three miles east along a wide gravel road at the base of the Panamint Range. Ballarat was hopefully named in 1890 after a town in Australia where the world's largest gold nugget had been found a year earlier. Today the CR Briggs Mine operates an open-pit gold mine several miles south of Ballarat. Miners and tourists stop at Ballarat to visit the rapidly deteriorating adobe ruins and buy cold drinks in a small store.

Panamint City, northeast of Ballarat up steep Surprise Canyon, came into being in 1873, when the search for the lost Breyfogle Mine led prospectors up the canyon. With riches in silver and copper, the town's slogan became "Richer than the Comstock."

The town was so rough and lawless that even Wells Fargo wouldn't handle the ore shipments. Mine owners were greatly concerned about a safe method of transporting the ore until Senator William M. Stewart, a partner in the mining venture, solved the problem by casting the bullion in 700-pound cannon balls and sending them out unguarded in an open express wagon. No bandit could cope with such a problem of seizure, transportation, and subsequent disposal, and until the

Panamint deposits were depleted in 1877, the town literally rolled its treasure down Surprise Canyon to the Carson City mint. In 1878 a cloudburst and flash flood carried the mineshaft timbers and parts of Panamint City's abodes down the canyon to the arid expanses of Panamint Sink.

Today the only remains are old stone walls, a few frame buildings, and some brick from the smoke stack that was part of the smelter.

To reach the remains of Panamint City, go two miles north of Ballarat and take Wingate Road, which branches off to the right to Surprise Canyon; drive four miles up the alluvial fan, park at Chris Wicht's camp, and hike six miles up the canyon. (One of the desert's many colorful characters, Wicht was a miner, saloon owner, and at one time the mayor of Ballarat.)

## In and Around Owens Valley

To the north, Owens Valley also provides excellent journeys into history. Olancha, located at the junction of U.S. 395 and California 190, began around 1861 as the site of a small mill. Later the town was a way station for the freight teams hauling Cerro Gordo ore. Thirty miles east of Olancha on California 190 is Darwin, a former mining town so close to the northern boundaries of the Navy's Coso Range that the town's water supply comes from within the confines of the base. The view of Panamint Valley, 12 miles away and 3,000 feet below the little community, is a rewarding part of the trip.

The town is named for Dr. Darwin French, whose party found and named Darwin Falls in 1860. After discovery of silver in the vicinity in 1874, Darwin soon had a population of 1,400. The town flourished for only two years, with little additional mining taking place until 1937-51, when the Darwin-Mt. Ophir Mine produced lead, silver, and zinc. The property is still maintained for potential future operations.

Cartago, at the southwestern tip of Owens Lake, was once a bustling port. During the 1870s steam paddle-wheelers, the

*Bessie Brady* and the *Molly Stevens*, steamed back and forth across the lake, carrying charcoal from two kilns on the west shore of the lake and 85-pound silver bars from the Cerro Gordo mines. Teamsters hauled these bars to Los Angeles, a three-week trip. According to the WPA guide to California, originally written in the 1930s, Cartago was "an employees' town, once considered a model housing project."

The historic town of Keeler is located on the east side of Owens Lake and may be reached via California 190 from

*Keeler*                                                        – *John Dunker*

Olancha or California 136 from Lone Pine. Keeler was involved in the mining, milling, shipping, woodcutting, and charcoal burning connected with Cerro Gordo that kept the shores of Owens Lake alive with activity in the early 1900s.

Many old houses and the Carson and Colorado Railroad depot can be seen in Keeler today, as can the ruins of the Sierra Talc Company mill that processed talc from local mines. At the end of Malone Street was a sizable Chinatown. In the hills behind Keeler are shacks and tunnels of small mines that produced gold, silver, and lead. North of the highway is a graveyard, much of which has been washed away by cloudbursts.

Cerro Gordo was given the name Fat Hill (or Big Hill) by Mexicans in 1865. The privately owned ghost town is now open April-October, weather permitting, for a picnic lunch and a $5-per-person guided tour or for a weekend retreat. Reservations are essential for overnight stays and helpful for day tours; call or fax (760) 876-5030.

Cerro Gordo is seven and a half picturesque miles east of Keeler on a road easily traveled by a four-wheel-drive vehicle, but navigable by nearly any vehicle in good shape, with adequate power, and a good spare tire, extra water, and ample fuel. The steep road gains about a mile in elevation and the going is slow, snaking through narrow canyons and tilted rock layers. The view across the valley is spectacular. Bring your camera and lots of film.

The road follows the approximate route of the famed Yellow Grade Road, constructed in 1868 and traveled by heavily laden mule teams making their way from the Cerro Gordo lode to the pueblo of Los Angeles, a village that grew to a city because of the commerce that flourished as a result of Cerro Gordo's riches.

In the mine's peak year, 1874, the Belshaw smelter turned out 300 silver-lead ingots (bullion bars) a day, and mule teams

*Belshaw smelter at Cerro Gordo*      *– Elizabeth Babcock*

made their laborious way down the steep road to Owens Lake's east shore with $2 million worth of bullion.

A smelter, the American Hotel, Belshaw House, a general-store museum, an assay-office museum, and a hoist house from the original mine at Cerro Gordo are among the structures still standing that can be seen on the tour.

On the northeast side of Owens Lake is Swansea, named after Swansea, Wales. Pure salt was sent from Saline Valley across the Inyo Mountains on a 14-mile tramway to the mill at Swansea. One of Cerro Gordo's smelters was also located here.

Today the site is marked with a historical plaque. Only the furnace (partially buried after a 1998 flash flood) and a boarded-up stone building remain.

*Manzanar*                                          *– Mark Pahuta*

Manzanar is located 12 miles north of Lone Pine on U.S. 395. When the Owens River fed this area, its rich farmland produced pears and apples (Manzanar is Spanish for "apple orchard"). A World War II relocation camp for Americans of Japanese ancestry, Manzanar was designated a National Historic Site in 1992. Two stone entrance markers to the west of the road mark the entrance to the camp where once more than 10,000 people were confined. Much of the site has been destroyed, but restoration work is under way.

A three-mile-long self-guided tour of the camp is available at the camp entrance. For a more detailed tour, pick up a booklet for a self-guided walking tour at the Eastern Sierra

Inter-Agency Visitor Center in Lone Pine or at the Eastern California Museum in Independence, five miles north of Manzanar. The museum also contains a poignant exhibit of possessions and photographs collected by former internees.

Each April the Manzanar Committee holds its annual pilgrimage, with former internees joining visitors in a moving ceremony of remembrance at Manzanar. Information about the next pilgrimage may be obtained by calling the committee, (323) 662-5102.

## Kern River Valley Area

Havilah may be reached by driving south along California 14, then west on California 178 over Walker Pass, and along Lake Isabella to Bodfish. Havilah and its ranger station are seven miles south of there on Bodfish-Caliente Road.

In 1864 gold was discovered in the area, and because of the ensuing rush, Havilah became the county seat when Kern County was created in 1866. As Bakersfield grew, the Havilah mines became increasingly difficult to work because of the high ground water level in the area. In 1872 Bakersfield became the county seat, and Havilah's population began to decline.

Havilah sights include a reconstructed courthouse with its historical museum (open weekends from 11 a.m. to 3 p.m.) and several cemeteries. Most of the graves are unmarked or weathered to illegibility, but some well-preserved gravestones remain. The town also has a picnic area.

Keysville, the first white settlers' community in Kern County, was a mining center from 1853 to 1870. A historical marker marks the site today. Keysville is located three miles west of Isabella and may be reached by a dirt road.

Keysville was named for Richard M. Keys, who discovered a rich gold ledge there in 1854. Like many mining towns, Keysville had an earlier name, "Hogeye" in this case.

The village, described as a community of "dingy dirt-floored shacks," was difficult to reach because of the surrounding Greenhorn Mountains. The first wagon to arrive in Keysville had to be lowered by a rope down the mountainside!

During the severe winters of 1861–63, Native Americans in Owens Valley raided white settlers' supplies to ward off starvation, thus starting a period of conflict. In April 1863, Captain Moses McLaughlin and his soldiers slaughtered 35 men of the Tubatulabal tribe, then marched over Walker Pass to Camp Independence. McLaughlin's report includes these chilling words, quoted in the book *In Historic Kern* (pages 113-114):

> I had been instructed by Colonel Jones to investigate the Indian troubles on Kern River. On arriving at Keysville I was waited upon by several of the residents of the place, who represented that there was a large body of Indians encamped upon the North Fork of Kern River; that many of these Indians had doubtless been engaged in the war and in the depredations committed in Kern River Valley; that Roberts and Waldron had lost about 150 head of stock; that many other citizens had lost cattle, horses and other property; that the roads were unsafe, and finally, that the Indians there congregated were for the most part strangers in the valley, and were thought to be Tehachapi and Owen's River Indians, who after seeing so many troops pass had endeavored to shield themselves from punishment by seeking the more immediate vicinity of the white settlements. …

> Accordingly at 2 a.m. on the 19th, accompanied by a detail of twenty men of my company and Lt. Daley, with Jose Chico as guide, I left camp, and at dawn surrounded the camp of the Indians, which was situated about ten miles from Keysville, upon the right bank of the Kern River. I had the bucks collected together, and informed Jose Chico and the citizens who had arrived that they might choose out those whom they knew to have been friendly. This was soon done. The boys and old men I sent back to their camps, and the

others, to the number of thirty-five, for whom no one could vouch, were either shot or sabered. Their only chance for life being their fleetness, but none escaped, though many of them fought well with knives, sticks, stones, and clubs. This extreme punishment, though I regret it, was necessary, and I feel certain that a few such examples will soon crush the Indians and finish the war in this and adjacent valleys. It is now a well-established fact that no treaty can be entered into with these Indians. They care nothing for pledges given, and have imagined that they could live better by war than peace. They will soon learn that they have been mistaken, as with the forces here they will soon either be killed off, or pushed so far in the surrounding deserts that they will perish by famine.

McLaughlin again crossed Indian Wells Valley in July 1863, this time to herd more than 900 captives from Owens Valley over Walker Pass to San Sebastian Reservation near Fort Tejon. The troubles subsided in late 1864 and early 1865, when only scattered uprisings upset the new settlers' orderly lives. The final clash occurred in 1867 near the Spanish mines at Coso.

*Windmill, Walker Pass*                                        *– Mark Pahuta*

# Part Two
# EXPLORING INDIAN WELLS VALLEY AND THE NORTHERN MOJAVE DESERT

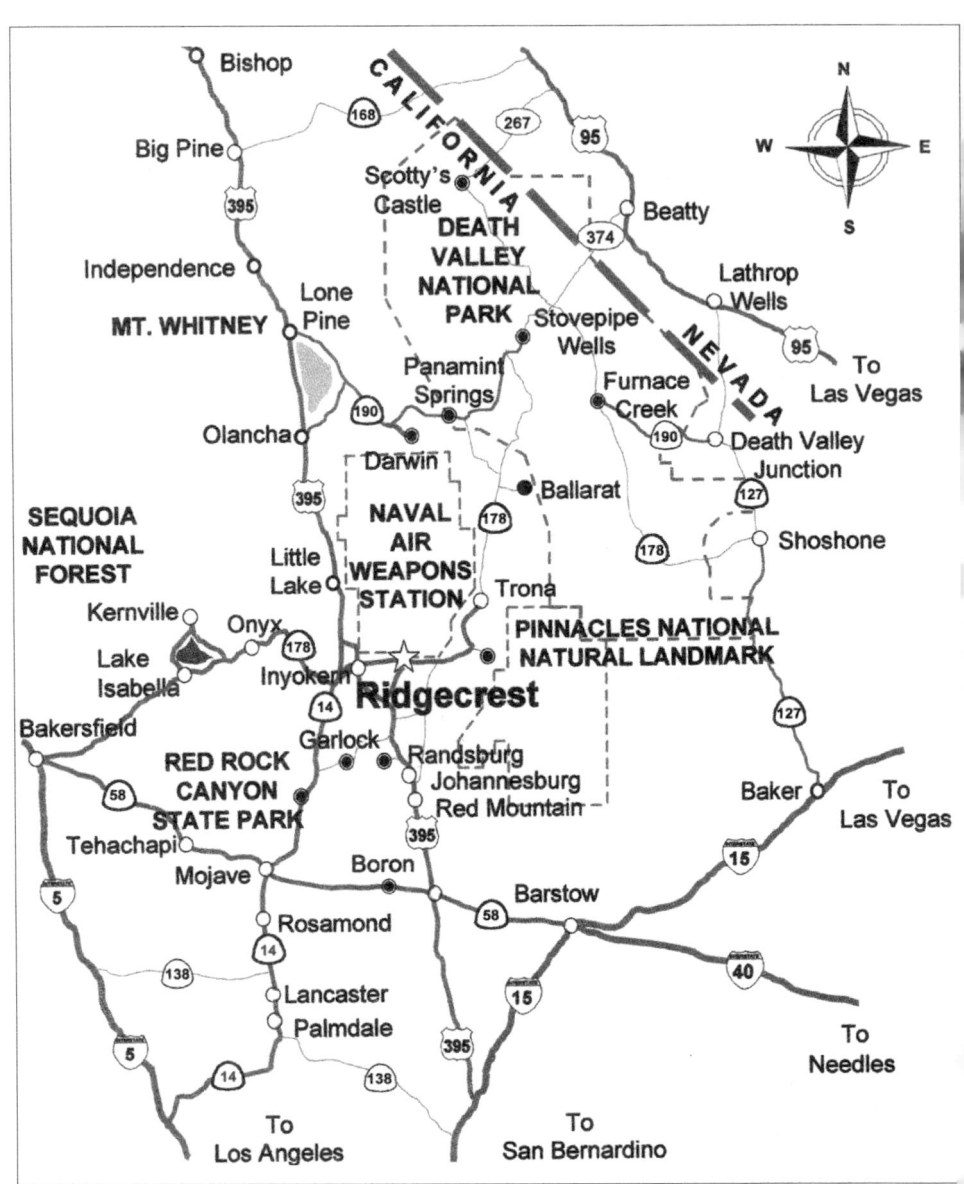

*Map of the area*

— *Lloyd Smith, Ph.D*

# SIGHTSEEING

Innumerable settlers and travelers — con men and thieves, drivers of wagon trains and logging trucks, shepherds and prospectors — have left their traces on the Indian Wells Valley, a high, sunny land at the northwestern end of the Mojave Desert. Within a day's journey are mountains, meadows, waterfalls, and sand dunes.

Local areas of historic, recreational, and scenic importance attract residents and tourists alike. Some suggestions for one-day trips are presented here with directions, indications of mileage, and brief descriptions of the attractions to be seen. Often the area is outside the borders of the valley, but has ties to our history or ecology.

This chapter is intended only as an introduction to this area. For more information about particular places, please refer to the pertinent books listed in our "Recommended Reading" section. In addition, participation in Cerro Coso Community College courses and seminars can give you informed entry to special places such as meadows of wildflowers, historic homesteads, and pioneer trails. Membership in some of the organizations listed in the back of this handbook can also offer many rewards.

Before setting out on any serious sightseeing or camping, check locally for wilderness permits, up-to-date road and weather conditions, and detailed maps. Since the 1994 passage of the California Desert Protection Act, our area has been undergoing major changes in terms of access to wilderness areas.

You are responsible for knowing what regulations pertain to the areas you plan to visit. For that reason, as well as for your own comfort and safety, you'll need the latest Bureau of Land Management or U.S. Forest Service maps pertaining to the areas you plan to visit. See the "Additional Sources of Information" section in the back of this book.

Please remember, too, that a change in altitude means a change in climate; extra clothing may come in handy. To increase the safety and comfort of your trip, always carry extra water and follow the other precautions listed in the "Safety Tips for the Desert Explorer" section.

## Good First Stops — Our Museums

The Indian Wells Valley is blessed with two museums, each with its own area of specialization and each offering a good introduction to that area. Both museum gift shops sell books pertinent to the local area, as well as souvenirs and gift items unique to our area.

The Maturango Museum offers an overview of the cultural and natural history of the Upper Mojave Desert, with an emphasis on the Indian Wells Valley. Be sure to look at the vestibule exhibit by the Historical Society of the Upper Mojave Desert, as well as the appealing exhibits for children.

*Maturango Museum with outdoor display of mining equipment*
*— Carroll Evans*

The gift shop has publications on the local area and a variety of beautiful arts and crafts. Be sure to ask about the educational tours. The museum, located at 100 E. Las Flores Ave. in Ridgecrest, is open from 10 a.m. to 5 p.m. seven days a week. The phone number is (760) 375-6900.

The U.S. Naval Museum of Armament and Technology is full of intriguing technology and fascinating history that will introduce you to the contributions China Lake and the Navy have made to the defense of the nation.

The museum's gift shop stocks T-shirts, coffee mugs, and other items bearing China Lake logos, as well as books, videos, aircraft and ship models, and much more.

The museum, which is open Mondays-Fridays, 10 a.m. to 4 p.m., is located on One Pearl Harbor Way, China Lake, and is accessible with a pass. If you are an American citizen, a guest pass is easy to obtain and well worth the effort. For further information, call the museum at (760) 939-3530.

## Sierra Canyons of Indian Wells Valley

Indian Wells, Short, Grapevine, and Sand Canyons, all within an hour's drive of the China Lake–Ridgecrest area, are pleasant spots for exploring or picnicking.

You may especially enjoy visiting in springtime, when the canyons offer entire mountainsides of desert wildflowers in bloom.

Most of the roads up these canyons can be negotiated by a passenger car, although washouts and rockfalls may make driving hazardous after a rainstorm.

The Owens Peak Wilderness Area limits exploration of the upper parts of these canyons to hiking. Motorized vehicles found in wilderness areas are subject to fines, so be careful to watch for signs indicating "Wilderness" or "Closed Road."

## Indian Wells Canyon

A historical marker in front of the Indian Wells Lodge, 2565 N. Highway 14, tells the story of the old Indian Wells water hole, site of the first water reached by members of the Jayhawker party of 1849 after their escape from Death Valley. North of the marker about a tenth of a mile is a dirt road leading west through Indian Wells Canyon toward Owens Peak. The first two and four-tenths miles of the road are wide and well-graded; six-tenths of a mile after that, permissible travel by automobile ends at the border of the Owens Peak Wilderness. The trail that continues into the wilderness offers hikers access to Owens Peak and the Pacific Crest Trail.

## Short Canyon

A trip to Short Canyon provides a delightful surprise for the desert visitor — a waterfall is found there in the springtime. Watercress and willows grow beside a small stream that flows down from the mountains, tumbles over a 20-foot drop, and then sinks into the sand below.

In years of abundant rainfall, wildflowers grow in profusion, but some flowers can be found here even when the rainfall has been scarce.

To reach Short Canyon, proceed northward on U.S. 395 to Leliter Road, about a mile north of the U.S. 395 and California 14 intersection. Turn left (west) off the highway and cross the frontage road onto the dirt Short Canyon road, which is directly across from Leliter Road and is marked with a Bureau of Land Management sign on the frontage road. Continue on the dirt road for half a mile, then turn left (south). After half a mile, turn right (west) again onto a road that leads over the hill to the stream.

The waterfall may be approached by following the stream bed and climbing a short distance over the rocks. The right fork of the road leads up the canyon to a parking area and a

*Joshua trees, Indian Wells Canyon*       *— Mark Pahuta*

favorite place to see springtime wildflowers. From the parking area, a good trail leads over the shoulder of a hill and up the stream bed.

## Grapevine Canyon

Grapevine Canyon takes its name from its wild grapevines and is one of the few local areas where the wild vines actually bear fruit. Approximately two miles north of the intersection of California 14 and U.S. 395, the road leading to the canyon goes west toward the mountains. After three miles, the road enters private property and is usually closed by a gate.

## Sand Canyon

Sand Canyon is a favorite spot for history- and nature-lovers. Travel north on U.S. 395 to the Brown Road exit, about five miles north of the junction of California 14 and U.S. 395. Turn west off the highway and cross the frontage road onto a dirt road that leads toward a gravel quarry.

Turn left in front of the quarry and follow the road past the quarry into the canyon. About two miles up the canyon from the highway, the road goes under a large pipe, part of a siphon on the Los Angeles aqueduct. Just beyond the pipe is a beautiful grove of cottonwood trees — just the spot for a family picnic.

The trailhead providing access to the Owens Peak Wilderness is three and one-tenth miles from the highway. The canyon offers hiking trails, primitive camping, and seasonal hunting. More than 100 bird species and more than 300 plant species have been observed in this remarkably varied canyon.

A special activity occurring every spring is the Sand Canyon Environmental Education Project (SEEP), in which the Bureau of Land Management (BLM) and eight other agencies in the Indian Wells Valley give every fifth grader in the valley a day-long experience of the canyon's environment and history.

## Nine-Mile Canyon to the Kern Plateau

The Kern Plateau and the surrounding territory comprise the principal summer recreation and fall hunting area quickly accessible to the Indian Wells Valley.

*Father and daughter on SEEP trip, Sand Canyon*
— *Elizabeth Babcock*

This extensive region, which ranges from semi-arid mountains to year-round running streams and deep fir forests, may be reached in an hour's drive up winding Nine-Mile Canyon.

On U.S. 395 almost 10 miles north of the intersection of U.S. 395 and California 14, a paved road, marked by a Kennedy Meadows sign, leads up the canyon west into the Sierra. A striking transition from desert to piñon forest occurs at the top of this grade. Some 12 miles from the highway, BLM has a summer fire station on the east side of the road. Immediately thereafter, the gravel Canebrake Road leads southwest to the Chimney Peak Back-Country Byway. Several camping areas may be reached via this road, which continues past the rustic Chimney Peak campground and through Lamont Meadow. Ultimately this byway joins the Walker Pass Road (California 178) near Canebrake.

The main road continues to the north, through typical piñon forest and past small meadows to an elevation of 7,540 feet, where you may look north and west into the High Sierra.

*Kern Plateau*                              *— Elizabeth Babcock*

The road then descends gently to the valley of the South Fork of the Kern River at about 6,000 feet.

After traversing an area with a number of private cabins on both sides, the road arrives at a major intersection 24 miles from U.S. 395. Continue on the road to the right for three miles to reach Kennedy Meadows Campground, an excellent campground for early-in-the-season fishing along the South Fork of the Kern River.

The road turning off to the left at the intersection will bring you to a country store offering groceries, sporting goods, ice, and other amenities. The store is usually open every day from the start of fishing season until well into deer season. The road crosses the South Fork of the Kern River shortly after leaving the store, then climbs past excellent campgrounds at Fish Creek and Troy Meadows. Both are on Fish Creek in a beautiful yellow-pine forest with dense stands of lodgepole pine in the valley bottoms. A pack station with saddle and pack animals for hire is on the right, just beyond Troy Meadows Campground.

The Bald Mountain Lookout Tower, approximately eight miles from Troy Meadows, offers a magnificent view of the Domelands Wilderness Area. If you wish to visit this fire tower, inquire at the Blackrock Information Station, located north of the major intersection.

The road continues south from the intersection toward Bald Mountain, then southwest over Sherman Pass and down to the Kern River and Kernville. The road north from Blackrock Station continues eight miles to Blackrock Pass and access by trail to the Golden Trout Wilderness Area. This beautiful loop drive from Ridgecrest up Nine-Mile Canyon to Kennedy Meadows, then to Blackrock, Sherman Pass, and Kernville is about 160 miles long and takes about four hours to drive.

Trails from this road lead to many pleasant streams and meadows and on beyond to the High Sierra. Depending on winter snow, the Kern Plateau is usually accessible to passenger cars from late April until early November.

## China Lake Range Areas

The historic and archaeological treasures within the boundaries of the Naval Air Weapons Station are protected under the supervision of the U.S. Navy. Specialists in geology,

*Big Petroglyph Canyon*                              *– Mark Pahuta*

archaeology, and zoology ensure that the environment is preserved against vandalism and environmental degradation. Military needs come first at China Lake; as a result, some of the best-preserved historical and scenic areas of the region are generally unavailable to the public.

## *Big and Little Petroglyph Canyons*

In May 1964, the U.S. Department of the Interior designated Petroglyph and Renegade Canyons (known today as Big and Little Petroglyph Canyons) a National Historical Monument, thereby bringing official recognition to the tremendous number and unique character of the Coso Range petroglyphs, which experts refer to as one of the world's greatest collections of rock art.

Petroglyphs are figures or symbols that are pecked, scratched, carved, or otherwise engraved into the surface of rocks and boulders, while pictographs, rarer in this vicinity, are designs painted on the rock.

Native American themes depicted on the canyon walls include hunters with bows and arrows shooting bighorn sheep; men with atlatls (spears), which were used before the introduction of the bow and arrow; men and dogs (or cats) attacking sheep; and many, many sheep and abstract geometrical designs. These petroglyphs are believed to have been created by shamans (medicine men) as part of their ceremonial rituals or "vision quests."

These petroglyphs are within the boundaries of the Naval Air Weapons Station, and when Navy security considerations permit, spring and fall tours of Little Petroglyph Canyon may be arranged through the China Lake Public Affairs Office. These tours must be led by trained, command-approved escorts. The Maturango Museum is the most well-known of the nonprofit organizations that coordinate and conduct petroglyph tours.

## Rose Valley

### Little Lake

Little Lake is approximately 30 miles northwest of Indian Wells Valley on U.S. 395. The property is privately owned and managed as a hunting club. The Owens River carved a gorge at the base of a great lava flow here on its way from Owens Lake to China Lake. Located on a flyway for many migrating birds, the waters at the highway's edge can provide interesting opportunities for bird-watchers. The hotel that formerly stood on the west side of the highway was destroyed by fire in the mid-1990s.

### Fossil Falls

North of Little Lake is Fossil Falls, the result of volcanic eruptions that occurred as recently as 20,000 years ago. After

*Fossil Falls*                                          *— Mark Pahuta*

lava poured into the Owens River channel, the water of the
river smoothed and polished this basaltic rock, forming the
sculptured features of Fossil Falls. At the head of each of the
falls are hollows varying in depth from two to 10 feet. In some
instances, tunnels have been worn between the hollows. The
resulting water-smoothed shapes are strangely pleasing to the
eye.

Prehistoric occupation of the Fossil Falls area probably varied over time in conjunction with climatic changes. Archaeologists believe that most of the archaeological remains present in the vicinity date from between about 6,000 years ago and the 19th century.

Rock rings made to support brush or reeds for temporary shelters may be found, as well as metates, hollowed-out areas used for seed grinding. Obsidian, widely used for arrow points and other tools, may also be found here.

Please remember that all such archaeological remains are protected by law, with stiff penalties for removing or disturbing any of these remains.

To reach Fossil Falls, go north on U.S. 395. The falls are three miles north of Little Lake and the site of the old Little Lake Hotel. Turn to the right (east) on Cinder Road just before the prominent cinder cone beside the highway. The cinders of this cone are mined for use as decorative rock, ballast, and other commercial products.

After six-tenths of a mile, take the right (south) fork of the road; then, in two-tenths of a mile take the left (southeast) fork; the other fork is marked "Not a Through Road." After three-tenths of a mile, the road ends in a parking area.

A well-marked trail starting at the southeast edge of the parking area leads for about a quarter of a mile over the lava flow to the top of the falls.

## Ayers Rock

Most local examples of Native American rock art are petroglyphs, but a few pictographs (rock paintings) may also be found. A short trip to Ayers Rock will give you the opportunity to see paintings of shamans, bighorn sheep, handprints, and other designs. The pictographs were probably made as recently as the early 20th century, perhaps by Bob Rabbit, the last Coso rain shaman.

To reach Ayers Rock, go north on U.S. 395 about five miles beyond Cinder Road to the Coso Junction Rest Stop. Turn right (east) onto Coso Road. After about three and seven-tenths miles, turn north (left) onto a smaller dirt road. Approximately four and three-tenths miles along this second road, you'll find a locked gate; a smaller dirt road to the left of the gate leads you to a parking loop and a marked quarter-mile trail to Ayers Rock.

The pictographs are fragile, so please be careful not to touch them, apply materials to facilitate photography, or do anything else that might cause damage.

## Owens Valley

Approximately an hour's drive north of Indian Wells Valley on U.S. 395 you'll reach scenic Owens Valley and the magnificent High Sierra, containing many lofty peaks, several more than 14,000 feet high.

Owens Valley abounds with points of historical and geological interest. Essentially a desert area between the Sierra Nevada on the west and the White and Inyo Mountains on the east, the valley stretches from its southern end below Olancha more than 80 miles north to Bishop.

Owens Valley has been lyrically described in Mary Austin's famous book, *Land of Little Rain*. The Owens River at one time coursed through the valley, terminating in Owens Lake, south of Lone Pine. Since the sale of water rights in the 1920s to the City of Los Angeles Department of Water and Power, the lake has become dry.

Each of the towns of Owens Valley has one or more roads snaking up to trailheads leading to the beauty, adventure, and inspiration of the Sierra wilderness. A few roadheads are described briefly here, but only guidebooks devoted to the Sierra Nevada can do justice to the many high-country adventures accessible from the Owens Valley.

## *Olancha and Olancha Falls*

The pastoral town of Olancha offers a starting point for several Owens Valley adventures. One such trip can take you on a historic loop around Owens Lake. From U.S. 395 north, turn east on California 190 at Olancha, then turn north on California 136 toward Lone Pine. Refer to "Old Towns With a Colorful Past" for information about Keeler, Swansea, and Cerro Gordo, all of which may be found near this route.

*Olancha Falls*  *— Dr. Bill Ferguson*

The Olancha Sand Dunes, a favorite site for motion-picture and television productions, may be found at the south end of the lakebed.

A trip to Olancha Falls is one of the many pleasant Sierra scrambles near Olancha. The road to the falls is rough, but navigable by a carefully driven passenger car. The road starts a mile and a tenth south of Gus's Fresh Jerky Shop on U.S. 395. Turn left (west) on a dirt road labeled "Walker Creek." After about four-tenths of a mile, take a left fork. You'll cross the aqueduct shortly thereafter.

Take two right forks in rapid succession, then continue west. After you've been on the dirt road for about a mile, it turns south. Half a mile further on, take another right fork west, cross under the power lines, and continue west to the National Forest boundary, where the road becomes Forest Service 19S01. After another two and four tenths miles, you'll reach a "T" intersection. Turn left (south), and continue less than half a mile to the line of trees. Park here and continue along the road on foot.

The road drops through the trees west across a small creek (Walker Creek) and after only about a tenth of a mile reaches the ruins of The Oaks Pack Station on Falls Creek — a lush, shady place for a picnic. The station operated in the 1930s, with the nearby cabins used as tourist vacation cottages. After the pack station closed, retired miners in the area lived in the cottages. Beyond The Oaks, a rocky trail leads west three-tenths of a mile up the canyon along the creek to the falls, which cascade over the rocks into a masonry basin.

## *Whitney Portal*

Whitney Portal is accessible from U.S. 395 at Lone Pine, about 80 miles north of Indian Wells Valley. A good stop along the way is the Eastern Sierra Inter-Agency Visitor Center just to the south of Lone Pine. The center offers much useful literature about the area, as well as an excellent view of Mount Whitney (elevation 14,492 feet), the highest peak in the contiguous 48 states.

At the center of Lone Pine is a sign designating the Alabama Hills. Turn left (west) onto the Whitney Portal road, which winds 13 miles up into the mountains. Whitney Portal, with its towering granitic cliffs, majestic pine trees, and

*Alabama Hills and Mount Whitney* — *Dolph Amster*

beautiful waterfall and pool, is a favorite picnic and camping spot. The high altitude makes the site a comfortably cool destination for a summer trip. A picnic area is at the base of the 10-and-a-half-mile trail to the top of Mount Whitney. The trail is clearly marked and requires no mountaineering skill, but hikers need stamina and the ability to withstand high altitudes.

Each summer, crowds of hikers seek to climb this famous trail. For that reason, the Forest Service requires permits for overnight use, as well as for day use above Lone Pine Lake. Call the Mt. Whitney Ranger Station in Lone Pine, (760) 876-6200, for further information.

## Alabama Hills

During the Civil War, Confederate sympathizers discovered placer gold (particles of gold found in superficial

*Alabama Hills rock formation*                    *— Dolph Amster*

deposits) in these hills and named them for a famous
Confederate cruiser, the *Alabama*.

Formed of granitic rock like their neighbors to the west,
the Alabama Hills are molded by a desert environment, which
gives them a very different appearance from the moister Sierra
peaks. These hills have been the setting for many movies and
television shows. Drive about six miles north of Lone Pine

and turn left (west) off U.S. 395 to the "Alabama Hills Scenic Route," an 18-mile loop along "Movie Road," which will take you through country oddly familiar to anyone who loves old Westerns.

The hills offer many possibilities for picnics (bring plenty of water) and exploring. Summers are hot, but the weather is pleasant during the other seasons. Check locally for information concerning the annual film festival, which features movie memorabilia and visits by surviving stars of the old Westerns.

## Horseshoe Meadow

The Horseshoe Meadow road leads to the trailhead for the Cottonwood Lakes Basin, an excellent destination for hikers and fishermen alike. To reach the trailhead, travel to Lone Pine on U.S. 395. At the center of town, turn west (left) onto the Whitney Portal Road. Drive three and two-tenths miles, then veer left at a sign for Horseshoe Meadow.

After a twisting, steep 19 and three-tenths miles on the paved Horseshoe Meadow road, turn right by a sign for the Cottonwood Lakes trailhead. After about half a mile, you'll reach a paved parking area from which you can easily hike to the Golden Trout Wilderness.

## Mount Whitney Fish Hatchery

About two miles north of Independence, a sign marks the Mount Whitney State Fish Hatchery road which turns left (west) up Oak Creek from U.S. 395.

The imposing fish-hatchery building, completed in 1917, was designed to reflect the grandeur and permanence of the mountains. The facility originally produced trout fingerlings for planting throughout the state. Today the hatchery produces 15 million golden, brown and rainbow trout eggs annually.

*Along the trail to Kearsarge Pass*                    — *Gary Babcock*

The beautiful grounds of the hatchery make it an enjoyable place to picnic at the tables provided. The public is welcome to stroll beside the large outdoor fish pools and to visit the hatchery any day from 8 a.m. to 4 p.m.

## Onion Valley

The road turning west from Independence and climbing the canyon of Independence Creek ends at Onion Valley, a cool, beautiful summer picnic and camping spot.

The four-and-a-half-mile trail from Onion Valley to Kearsarge Pass is one of the easiest and most rewarding in the Sierra and makes a good introductory hike for unacclimated newcomers.

Several lovely mountain lakes are found near the trail, and the view from Kearsarge Pass is one of nature's miracles.

## Big Pine Creek

Palisades Glacier, the largest glacier in the Sierra, is accessible to ambitious hikers by trail from the Big Pine Creek roadhead 11 miles west of the town of Big Pine on Crocker Street. The trail is very popular, so call (760) 873-2483 to obtain a wilderness permit before you go.

The area, favored by mountaineers, hikers, and fishermen, is at an altitude that makes it cool and pleasant during the summer months.

To see the glacier and the towering peaks of the Palisades above it, a strenuous five-mile hike to Fourth Lake is required. The glacier itself is two and a half miles beyond.

# White Mountains

The White Mountains form a dramatic eastern boundary to Owens Valley. Although many natural attractions are found in this area, we have limited our selection to the one most popular with Indian Wells Valley residents.

## Bristlecone Pine Forest

The high, dry mountains located on the east side of Owens Valley are the site of the oldest known living trees, the bristlecone pines. Located at elevations between 8,500 and 11,700 feet, hundreds of these pines, sandblasted for thousands of years, raise gnarled trunks above the white rock. The oldest specimen is more than 4,700 years old.

The best time to visit this area is during July, August, and early September. Take water, warm clothing, sunscreen, and a hat.

Drive north on U.S. 395 and turn east (right) half a mile past Big Pine on California 168; continue to the top of Westgard Pass (elevation 7,814 feet). Thirteen miles from Big Pine, turn

*Bristlecone pines*                           *– William Fettkether*

north (left) at the large sign giving Bristlecone Forest directions. Approximately 10 miles of steep, paved road leads to Schulman Grove, named as a memorial to Dr. Edmund Schulman, who discovered the great age of the trees.

If you pause at Sierra Viewpoint on this road, you can see across the valley 13 of the 15 highest peaks in California. Regular passenger cars have no trouble with the main road; four-wheel-drive vehicles are needed for side roads.

The visitor center includes picnic areas, restrooms, outdoor exhibits, and two self-guided nature trails. To help defray expenses, the Forest Service charges modest fees for use of these facilities. A two-mile walk within the grove brings you to the world's oldest tree, the 4,723-year-old Methuselah tree. To help provide protection against vandalism, the oldest trees are not identified.

Drive 12 miles beyond the Schulman Grove on a good dirt road to see the Patriarch pine, only 1,500 years old, but still, at 36 feet eight inches in circumference, the largest known bristlecone pine.

The road ends after two more miles at a locked gate. A road goes seven miles farther to the top of White Mountain (elevation 14,246 feet), which is higher than all the Sierra peaks except Mount Whitney and Mount Williamson.

Perched atop the peak is the White Mountain Research Station's Summit Facility, the highest high-elevation research station in North America. Established in 1950 by the Naval Ordnance Test Station at China Lake, the research station is now owned and run by the University of California.

## East Through Searles Valley

California 178 (Trona Road) takes you east from Ridgecrest to the scenic wonders of Searles, Panamint, and Death Valleys.

But before you leave the Indian Wells Valley, you might enjoy a short visit to the Ridgecrest Regional Wild Horse and Burro Corrals maintained by BLM just three miles east of Ridgecrest.

At the top of the rise, turn right onto the Randsburg Wash Road; the corral is immediately to the right. The animals housed here have been gathered from various southwestern sites, including China Lake ranges.

BLM holds the animals in its corrals for adoption at regularly scheduled auctions. Business hours are weekdays 7:30 a.m.-4 p.m., and visitors are welcome.

*Trona Pinnacles* — *Mark Pahuta*

On your way to Trona through Poison Canyon, keep a sharp eye out along the left (north) side of the road to see Fish Rock, a popular piece of local artwork that turns a large roadside rock into a many-toothed monster. Also to be found in Poison Canyon are fossil clams and snails, pressed into the mud of the lake that covered the area between 20,000 and 50,000 years ago.

## Trona Pinnacles

The dirt road to the Trona Pinnacles National Natural Landmark turns off Trona Road to the right (south) almost 16 miles east of the China Lake south gate. Follow the signs as you turn off the highway toward the pinnacles.

The ground becomes "self-rising," a phenomenon caused by capillary action that brings a porous mixture of salts and clay to the surface, thus causing the spongy higher ground. After about two miles, the road dips down off the self-rising ground, and two and a half miles from there (five and a half miles from the Trona road) are the pinnacles.

These geological oddities are believed to have been formed in Searles Lake sometime during the wet Tioga Glacial Stage, 10,000 to 23,000 years ago. Calcareous tufa deposits formed the pinnacles, the tallest of which is between 100 and 140 feet high. The deposits have porous central channels through which springs flowed when Searles Lake covered the area.

A loop trail through the formations allows you to get a close look. Please stay on the trail to avoid defacing the pinnacles. These wonders of nature are spectacular at any time; at sunrise or moonrise they're unforgettable.

A favorite location for film and TV productions, the pinnacles have doubled as alien landscapes in such productions as "Dinosaurs," "Star Trek V," "The Planet of the Apes," and more.

Ridgecrest often becomes headquarters for film and video location shoots, which help the local economy and lend an air of glamour to the high desert.

*Ridgecrest Film Commissioner Ray Arthur, flanked by "ER" stars George Clooney (left) and Anthony Edwards during location shooting at the Trona Pinnacles*
*— Ridgecrest Film Commission*

## *Searles Lake*

Along the shores of the Searles Lake playa, about 25 miles east of Ridgecrest on California 178 (Trona Road), are the neighboring communities of Argus, Westend, Trona, and Pioneer Point.

Trona was named for the white chemical salt trona, mined from the lake since 1916. Other products from Searles Lake are potash, soda ash, borax, saltcake, lithium, and bromine.

The annual Gem-O-Rama of the Searles Lake Gem and Mineral Society offers a good way to learn more about the fascinating history and resources of Searles Lake. Held during the second weekend in October for more than 60 years, the show includes plant tours and mineral-collection trips, set up in cooperation with IMC Chemicals, Inc.

## Panamint Valley

The shortest route to Death Valley is by way of Trona and Panamint Valley. About 15 miles north of Trona, the road reaches Slate Range Crossing. Here is a spectacular view of the entire Panamint Valley enclosed by the Argus Mountains on the west and by the magnificent Panamints, dominated by towering Telescope Peak, on the east.

A few yards south of the Slate Range Crossing vista point, California 178 crosses a narrow dirt road that winds down to the valley floor and continues along the length of the valley. This road is the famed Nadeau Trail, named for Remi Nadeau, who built it to haul supplies to the valley's silver mines.

## *Darwin Falls*

Darwin Falls, located in Panamint Valley, is a true desert oasis. Water trickles beneath gravel for miles to emerge and

*Darwin Falls*                                              *— Mark Pahuta*

splash down a ridge of resistant rock, forming upper and lower Darwin Falls.

In the overhang beside the lower falls, wonderfully green hanging ferns grow, along with wild celery and watercress. In the spring and summer there are beautiful flowers and lush grass, cattails, reeds, and butterflies.

To reach Darwin Falls, travel about 46 miles beyond Trona via California 178 north and California 190 west to Panamint Springs. A mile west of Panamint Springs, turn to the left onto a road running up a dry wash. In about two and a half miles is an intersection, with the left road going to Darwin and the road to Darwin Falls continuing on straight ahead.

Park near the intersection and continue along a trail following the stream. After about a mile, the trail arrives at the base of the falls. Climbing to the upper falls involves some rock scrambling, but the lower falls are relatively easy to reach.

## Death Valley National Park

Newcomers to the area have undoubtedly heard many tales of the vast and varied land that is Death Valley National Park. Some may recognize the name from hearing about the harshness of a climate where summer temperatures have reached an official high of 134 degrees, with ground temperatures 10 degrees higher or more.

In recent years, tourists from Europe and Japan have flocked to Death Valley in air-conditioned vehicles to experience that extreme summer heat. More thousands of tourists have discovered how delightful Death Valley can be from late October to May, when the climate is warm and balmy.

The park, established as a national monument in 1933 and designated a national park in 1995, comprises more than 3.3 million acres of desert. There's a lot to see and do in Death Valley, so if a leisurely trip is not possible, you might decide to visit a small area of the park and make return trips to other areas. Distances are long between the many scenic and historic places of interest.

Whether your trip will be short or long, the Maturango Museum is a good first stop for maps, books, and handouts to enhance your enjoyment of your Death Valley visit. The

*Death Valley* *— Dolph Amster*

friendly museum staff can also help you with information about such matters as park fees, overnight accommodations, and weather and road conditions.

To reach Death Valley from Ridgecrest, travel east through Trona on California 178. You'll see beautiful Telescope Peak, highest mountain of the Panamint Range, as you cross the Slate Range and continue along the length of Panamint Valley. Ten miles after you pass the turnoff to Ballarat, the road branches, offering two ways to enter the park.

To go by way of scenic Towne Pass, turn left (northwest) onto Panamint Valley Road. After about 23 miles, you'll dead end on California 190. Turn right (east) toward the pass, about 12 miles away.

Also well worth exploring is Wildrose Road, the right-bearing route 10 miles north of the Ballarat turnoff. During some seasons, this road may be washed out, but if it's open, it

*Charcoal kilns at Mahogany Flat*              *— Historical Society*
                                              *of the Upper Mojave Desert*

offers magnificent rewards for the careful driver in a passenger vehicle in good condition. (The road is too narrow in spots to handle big rigs.)

Wildrose Road winds up through the Panamints, offering access to the historic Mahogany Flat charcoal kilns. These kilns, operating in 1877-78, produced charcoal for silver-lead smelters in the Argus Range.

Emigrant Canyon Road, which continues northwest from Wildrose Road, offers side trips to a breathtaking view of Death Valley at Aguereberry Point and to the site of the former mining town of Skidoo. Descending steep Emigrant Canyon, this road joins California 190 at Emigrant Ranger Station in Death Valley.

History is much in evidence elsewhere in Death Valley National Park too. Among the interesting historic points to be found are the graves of Jim Dayton and Shorty Harris, the site of the Eagle Borax Works where Isador Daunet started the first borax operation, the remains of the Keane Wonder Mine, the ruins of the Old Harmony Mill, and other evidence of mining activity, lost mines, ghost towns, and railroads.

More recent history has left its mark on the valley too, with Scotty's Castle, Furnace Creek Inn, and (just outside the eastern boundary of the park) Amargosa Opera House at Death Valley Junction only three of the most popular attractions.

A popular belief is that the valley was named by a member of the band of emigrants who crossed the valley in 1849. The annual Death Valley '49ers Encampment, held in November, commemorates early days in the valley and the struggles of the pioneers to cross this hostile region.

## South to the El Paso Mountains

The El Paso Mountains, located south of Ridgecrest, are of special interest to rockhounds because agate, jasper, petrified wood, and other gem minerals may be found here. The mountains were home to numerous prospectors, miners, and other rugged individualists who left mines and other historic artifacts in the area.

Camera enthusiasts and artists will find subjects in the old cabins, brightly colored cliffs, and rock formations to be

*Amargosa Opera House, Death Valley Junction    — John Dunker*

*Doll-size bottle house at Mingus-Mead cabins, Bonanza Trail*
*— Elizabeth Babcock*

seen along the Bonanza Trail, a Bureau of Land Management concept centered in the El Pasos and encompassing sites in the Sierra Nevada, Panamint, and Inyo ranges.

The BLM Ridgecrest Field Office is working to provide interpretive signs documenting the lives and times of the early prospectors and miners who followed their dreams by chasing the lure of gold and other precious metals.

Most of the Bonanza Trail sites are located south of the El Paso Mountain Wilderness in rugged country accessible only to off-highway vehicles. Watch carefully for access signs to avoid straying into wilderness areas where vehicles are prohibited.

Several of the old cabins are maintained through BLM's Adopt-a-Cabin Program, wherein volunteers maintain the cabins and BLM provides needed materials.

The cabins are available for overnight dry camping on a first-come, first-served basis. For further information, contact the BLM Ridgecrest Field Office, (760) 384-5400.

## Garlock Fault

The Garlock Fault, where it runs through the Cantil Valley south of Ridgecrest, presents typical surface features associated with earthquake faults.

The Cantil Valley is a closed basin between the El Paso and Rand mountains. The valley probably was formed by the rising of the mountains along the Garlock fault, with a subsequent down-drop (sinking) of the valley.

The fault is traceable some 150 miles from its junction with the San Andreas Fault south of Bakersfield northeast to the Avawatz Mountains northwest of Baker.

Proceed south from Ridgecrest to Cantil Valley via U.S. 395. You will cross the main Garlock fault trace eight and a half miles south of the junction of China Lake Boulevard with U.S. 395. Two-tenths of a mile beyond this trace, an offset stream bed may be seen if you walk up a wash to the right (west) of U.S. 395. Where the wash makes a sudden jog to the left, the ground has moved to form the offset.

To see more of the fault, take the Garlock Road to the right. Beginning just south of the ghost town of Garlock is a fault scarp running approximately parallel to the road for two miles. Notice how erosion is rounding off the abrupt face of the scarp. An investigation of this scarp near the town of Garlock in 1909 gave the fault its name.

## Mesquite and Last Chance Canyons

To reach the Last Chance Canyon area, travel south on U.S. 395 for about eight and a half miles and take the road that turns off to Garlock.

About a mile and a half beyond Garlock, take the dirt road to the right through Mesquite and Last Chance Canyons. This loop trip of about 14 miles is part of the Bonanza Trail and comes out on the Garlock Road west of Saltdale.

Because the road through Last Chance Canyon traverses a stream bed at numerous points, it is not wise to enter the canyon in bad weather or just after a storm. Four-wheel-drive or high-clearance vehicles are advisable.

You'll pass many gold, copper, lead, and silver mining claims. Perhaps the most famous was the home of Burro Schmidt, one of the best-known of the colorful characters making the El Pasos their home.

Schmidt was a man with a mission. After he realized that packing ore over the mountain from his claim in Last Chance

Canyon would be difficult, he began his famed tunnel through the mountain.

Soon he was obsessed with digging through to the other side.

He worked alone for many years to blast through about half a mile of solid rock until at last he reached daylight on the other side of the mountain.

*Burro Schmidt getting a haircut outside his cabin.        — Maturango Museum*

Local legend has it that after he finished the task, he lost interest in his prospecting and simply left!

Today the tunnel's owner charges a small fee to let you walk in Burro Schmidt's path. The tunnel is about 2,000 feet long and is safe to visit.

Bring flashlights and wear comfortable, thick-soled shoes. Be careful as you walk through — the tunnel is too low for six-footers to walk upright in some places.

Your reward will be well worth the short hike. At the end of the tunnel, you'll get a spectacular view for hundreds of miles in all directions.

# South Along California 14

## *Black Mountain*

Black Mountain, a 5,259-foot extinct volcano, looms on Indian Wells Valley's southwestern horizon, just north of the El Paso Mountains.

The romantic aura of Black Mountain is due in part to its identification with many local Native American groups; the mountain was considered a sacred site for nomadic tribes from as far away as Utah. Artifacts such as grinding stones, tools, and pictographs have been found.

Obsidian chips, found at many Native American gathering sites in the area, are intriguing because obsidian does not naturally occur on Black Mountain.

Please be careful not to touch or remove any artifacts you may find. All historic and archaeological sites on public lands are protected by law, with severe penalties for damaging or otherwise harming public resources.

The mountain is located within the El Paso Mountain Wilderness and is open to hikers and horses only. No motorized vehicles are allowed. The area is home to many species of wildlife including bobcats, cottontail rabbits, chukkars, snakes, and rodents.

## *Red Rock Canyon State Park*

In Red Rock Canyon on California 14, approximately 35 miles southwest of Ridgecrest, are magnificent cliffs that have been eroded into fantastic shapes. The beautiful coloring of these formations is made more brilliant by early morning or late afternoon sunlight.

Natural preserves have been set aside within the park to protect the unique geology, vegetation, and wildlife. Many

*Red Rock Canyon*                                                          *— Mark Pahuta*

trails are now closed to off-road vehicles, but hiking is permitted except where it would threaten the cliff-nesting birds of prey during nesting season.

In an earlier era, members of Kaiwaiisu tribes traveled in small groups and lived in the canyon. Today the canyon is a popular attraction for tourists, campers, and photographers. Movie buffs will recognize scenes from "Jurassic Park" and many other film and TV productions.

The canyon's visitor center at Ricardo Campground welcomes newcomers and longtime residents alike, as displays, furnishings, and programs are added. Some of the Miocene-era fossils that have been found in the canyon's Ricardo Formation are on display at the visitor center.

Road and trail access changes as the park is upgraded. Call (661) 942-0662 for further information.

## Desert Tortoise Natural Area

The desert tortoise (*Gopherus agassizi*) is the official California State Reptile. One of the best places to learn about this long-lived but surprisingly fragile creature is the Desert Tortoise Natural Area, which has one of the highest known densities of desert tortoises per square mile.

Located five and a half miles northeast of California City on the Randsburg–Mojave Road, the preserve is managed by BLM, which closed the public land to vehicle use in 1975. You may explore the hiking trails and interpretive kiosks.

The best time to visit is mid-March to mid-June; in other months the tortoises tend to stay inside their burrows.

To protect the desert tortoise from the onslaught of civilization, the Desert Tortoise Preserve Committee has coordinated the installation of low, woven-wire fencing along

*Desert tortoise*                                    *– Griff Davies*

portions of California 58 and other roads in the vicinity of the natural area.

## Walker Pass and Beyond

Walker Pass, the most southerly of the passes through the Sierra, was named for Joseph Reddeford Walker, an experienced and capable guide and trapper, who discovered this route through the mountains in 1834 while leading an expedition from Monterey to the Owens Valley.

Take California 14 to California 178 West, three miles south of the California 178 East turnoff to Inyokern. Turn right (west) and continue eight miles to the pass (elevation 5,250 feet). The distinctive rock formation visible to the south of the road en route to Walker Pass is Robbers' Roost, which sheltered the bandit Tiburcio Vasquez as he waited to rob travelers.

Today, this granite complex of crevices and caves shelters many kinds of raptors, including the red-tailed hawk. (The area is closed to motor vehicles between February 1 and July 1 each year to allow the raptors undisturbed nesting time.) The area on both sides of the pass is especially beautiful in the winter just after a snowstorm when the many Joshua trees are snow-covered and in the spring when the Joshua trees and wildflowers are in bloom.

The Pacific Crest Trail winds through the mountains to the west of the Indian Wells Valley, offering several access points for one-day hikes. A good place to join the trail is at Walker Pass, where you can move north along a path that begins with a relatively steep climb, then soon evens out. You can see a wonderful view of the Indian Wells Valley from about five miles up the trail.

## Onyx

If you like meadowlands, you'll like the California 178 drive beyond Walker Pass along the South Fork of the Kern River. The road goes through green pastureland dotted with large cottonwood trees and through Onyx, home of the colorful

*Onyx Store* — *Mark Pahuta*

old Onyx Store, established in 1851 and, until its recent closure, reported to be the oldest continuously operating store in California.

## Kern River Preserve

Just beyond Onyx are Weldon and Audubon California's Kern River Preserve, a 1,300-acre habitat that contains one of the largest and finest remaining stands of cottonwood-willow streamside forests in California. More than 330 species of birds

*Cottonwood at Kern River Preserve*                    *– Gary Babcock*

and 130 species of butterflies have been seen here. A well-marked self-guided trail meanders through the preserve.

A Turkey Vulture Festival occurs each fall to celebrate North America's largest known concentration of turkey vultures during migration. In spring the Kern Valley Bioregions Festival celebrates the area's biological diversity.

The preserve is located approximately 30 miles from the California 14 junction with California 178 West. You'll find the turnoff to the preserve on the west side of Weldon, six tenths of a mile beyond the South Fork Elementary School and only 100 yards past Kelso Valley Road. On the right is a large sign for the preserve. Turn right onto a dirt road. The entry to the preserve is on private land, so drive slowly so as not to disturb the cattle. The preserve is open from dawn to dusk every day of the year, including holidays.

## Piute Mountains

Pine trees, green meadows, and wildflowers add to the soft beauty of the Piute Mountains. Turn onto the Kelso Valley Road turnoff left (south) eight-tenths of a mile west of the Weldon Post Office. A paved road leads 20 miles to a junction; then a graded dirt road continues toward the right (west) nine and a half miles up to the site of Claraville (elevation 6,300 feet). This community's last building, constructed in the 1860s, has been dismantled and reconstructed at Bakersfield's Pioneer Village.

French Meadow is the best known of the Piute Mountains' pretty meadows nestled in the timber.

A trip through one of the canyons described below could form a pleasant homeward leg on a loop trip to the Kern River area.

The Jawbone Canyon route is the longest and easiest. Drive 20 miles past the Weldon turnoff to the Piute Mountains and turn left (south) onto the Kelso Valley Road; continue for a mile and three-tenths. Turn left again and go east through Butterbredt Canyon for 15 miles along a graded dirt road to Jawbone Canyon, then six miles on paved road to California 14. The Jawbone Canyon road comes out approximately two miles below (south) of Red Rock Canyon.

Bird Spring Canyon road starts at a point on Kelso Valley Road 11 and a half miles from the California 178 turnoff and winds 14 and a half miles over Bird Spring Pass (elevation 5,300 feet) to the same dirt road mentioned above.

Turn left (north) one and a half miles and then right (east) four and a half miles to California 14. A road also turns left (east) through Dove Springs Canyon 19 and a half miles from the Weldon turnoff. The road is not maintained and should be taken only by four-wheel-drive vehicles.

## Lake Isabella

The Isabella Dam, built and maintained by the U.S. Army Corps of Engineers, holds back the waters of the Kern River to form Lake Isabella, only about an hour's drive west of Ridgecrest. Boating, swimming, water skiing, and year-around fishing have made Lake Isabella a popular recreational area. Campgrounds and trailer sites, as well as landing docks, are available. Motels and restaurants are located around the lake in the towns of Lake Isabella, Wofford Heights, and Kernville.

## Kernville

The site of the original town of Kernville was flooded in 1951-53 as Lake Isabella formed behind the dam. New Kernville is to the north of the lake. Originally an Indian camp, the old town was first named Whiskey Flats during the gold rush, when it boasted a population of 5,000.

An annual celebration, Whiskey Flats Days, held in February, recalls the settlement's early days.

*Lake Isabella*                                        *— Mark Pahuta*

With its cozy inns, beautiful surroundings, and local arts and crafts, Kernville is a great choice for a relaxing day or a weekend. Be sure to visit the Kern Valley Museum, run by the Kern River Valley Historical Society. The museum is located at 49 Big Blue Road (next to the post office) and is open from 10 a.m. to 4 p.m. Thursdays through Saturdays.

A well-marked turnoff (north) to Kernville is just past Weldon approximately thirty-two miles west of the intersection of California 14 and California 178 West. You can drive around the lake by going through Kernville and Wofford Heights to the town of Lake Isabella, where you rejoin California 178.

## *Kern Canyon*

North of Kernville, the Kern River flows through a picturesque canyon, with many picnic spots and campsites easily accessible from a good road along the east bank of the river. About 12 miles north of Kernville, 700-foot-high Salmon Creek Falls may be seen in the distance to the right of the road. Farther on, four miles beyond Road's End, beautiful South Creek Falls splashes over a cliff at the left side of the road.

## Sherman Pass Road

The Kern Plateau has been described as a gentle wilderness, for in contrast to the rugged peaks of the Sierra, it is a land of low, forested ridges, small trout streams, and delicate green meadows. The plateau's lower elevation makes it accessible for a longer season than is the Sierra.

You can enter the west side of the Kern Plateau by following the Kern River north of Kernville for 18 and a half miles and then turning right (east) onto the Sherman Pass road. As with any winding mountain road, take care to stay well over on your side of the road as you approach curves.

The road climbs steadily for five miles through digger pines and chaparral until the lovely pine-covered mountains ahead come into view. After two more miles, the road passes into the forest and wanders for miles through the pines and meadows. A campground is located at Horse Meadow.

About 37 miles from the Kern Canyon, the Sherman Pass road reaches a trail to the Domelands Wilderness Area. Church Dome (elevation 8,501 feet), the large granitic outcrop at the edge of the domelands, may be reached by hiking a mile and a half along this trail. The 62,561-acre Domelands Wilderness Area, established in 1963, is east of the main Kern River and northeast of Kernville and may also be reached by trail from Nine-Mile Canyon.

## Trail of a Hundred Giants

The lovely Trail of a Hundred Giants is one of the most popular hiking trails of Giant Sequoia National Monument. To reach this cathedral-like grove of giant sequoia trees, travel about 45 miles northwest of Kernville on State Mtn 50. After climbing quickly up from Johnsondale (formerly a lumber camp, now a privately owned resort), the road reaches a glorious viewpoint from which to see the high peaks to the north, as well as the surrounding countryside for many miles around.

You'll pass through a thick forest of incense cedars and Jeffrey and sugar pines. Much of this forest is now encompassed in Giant Sequoia National Monument, established in April 2000. When you reach the Western Divide Highway, turn right (north), and after two and a half miles, you'll reach the parking area.

The half-mile-long Trail of a Hundred Giants is located within the Long Meadow Giant Sequoia Grove, which encompasses 355 acres and contains 267 *Sequoia gigantea*, each more than 500 years old. The largest tree in the grove has reached an advanced old age of perhaps 1,500 years, as well as a diameter of 20 feet and a height of 220 feet.

## *Greenhorn Mountains*

Another beautiful forested drive has its starting point on the west side of Lake Isabella, four miles south of Kernville, at the turnoff to the Greenhorn Mountains. California 155 climbs steadily for about seven miles through scrub forest and then through cool, lush pines and cedars to Greenhorn Summit. Camping and hiking are favorite summer activities.

Shirley Meadows, about four miles south of the summit, is a favorite wintertime ski area. When there is sufficient snow, two chair lifts operate on weekends.

The road continues steeply down the west side of the mountains past several campsites to Glennville and other mining camps of historical interest.

*Red Rock Canyon*                                                                                          — *Mark Pahut*

# CAMPING

This section offers a selection of campsites available within a day's drive of Ridgecrest — wonderful places to establish your temporary outdoor home.

Late spring, summer, and fall are favorite times for experiencing the mountains, with the cooler seasons of the year offering good temperatures for desert hiking and camping in such beautiful spots as Fossil Falls and Red Rock Canyon State Park.

Sequoia National Forest is also an accessible site for one-day or weekend adventures. It is located at the southern end of the Sierra Nevada, extending from the Kings River on the north to the Tehachapi Mountains on the south. The eastern boundary includes the Sierra summit in places and reaches to the edges of the Mojave Desert in others. On the west, the forest extends to the brush-covered foothills bordering the San Joaquin Valley.

With elevations ranging from 1,000 feet in the foothills region to peaks over 14,000 feet high in the rugged High Sierra country, this area provides visitors with some of the most spectacular mountain views in the entire West. The high granite country is dotted with many secluded lakes and mountain meadows.

The forest is home to the monarch of the plant kingdom, the *Sequoia gigantea*. Within the forest are 39 sequoia groves, some including more than 100 of these beautiful trees. Thirty-three of the groves are found within the Giant Sequoia National Monument, created in April 2000.

Death Valley, with sand dunes, canyons, and sweeping views of stark desert and distant mountain peaks, easily matches the Sierra Nevada for majesty and beauty. From late fall through winter and into spring, Death Valley National Park

*Eastern Sierra*                                   *— Dolph Amster*

attracts hikers and campers. Death Valley campsites are not included in this chapter because information and maps are so easily acquired. The Maturango Museum in Ridgecrest is an excellent place to get the latest Death Valley information. Camping or hiking there in the summertime is not recommended because temperatures are dangerously high. Late fall, winter, and early spring are wonderful times to view Death Valley's grandeur.

Some differences exist between national forest and state park campgrounds. Some of the national forest campgrounds are remote and without potable water. Camping opportunities range from areas where you may camp anywhere (except where prohibitions are marked) to sites with piped water where you pay a small fee on the honor system. If you wish to camp in a remote area, away from civilization and crowds, national forest campgrounds are the answer.

Recreational facilities in the national forests and parks are constantly being upgraded, with new campsites added and old ones improved and enlarged with expanded recreational facilities. Because of this constant change, this chapter should be considered only a preliminary guide. We advise you to check with the appropriate information sources before your camping trip.

In recent years, California's campgrounds have become overcrowded, particularly on holiday weekends. To avoid disappointment, you should make reservations, if possible, and reach your destination as early as practicable. You should also be aware that fees accompany making reservations by phone. As of this writing, changes in fees are being contemplated in some areas. Also contemplated are closures in some areas because of environmental concerns.

## Day Hiking and Backpacking

Numerous trails into the wilderness offer another type of camping experience. Trails, including the Pacific Crest Trail, are easily accessible and marked. If you prefer not to carry your own pack, you can take a commercially operated pack trip.

Many experienced hikers say that the trails through the southern Sierra offer views and variety not ordinarily available in the more heavily forested northern parks. The dryer eastern slopes of the Sierra host smaller trees and shrubs than you will find at King's Canyon or Yosemite. The many areas of sparse vegetation on the eastern slopes will make your walking easier. The relatively dry climate also discourages mosquitoes and other insects, at least at lower elevations — a most welcome advantage.

Another major advantage to living in the Indian Wells Valley is the opportunity to take a mountain hike at almost a moment's notice. Some local residents have their own hiking and camping calendars — an annual birthday hike up nearby Owens Peak, perhaps, or an overnight trip to celebrate Easter each year. By fitting your destinations to the seasons, you can treat yourself to a variety of scenery.

Backpacking into the wilderness is a spectacular experience, with many miles of trails and beautiful country to see. Many of the campgrounds listed in this chapter are jumping off points for the Sierra back country.

If you are a newcomer to the mountains, careful planning is important. Good maps, lightweight equipment, appropriate clothing, and common sense are all necessary for a successful experience. Call the numbers listed below for information on permits.

Wherever you hike or camp, be sure to follow the basic rules of outdoor safety, as outlined in our "Safety Tips for the Desert Explorer" section. Good maps are a must.

## Camping in Ridgecrest

*Desert Empire Fairgrounds, Ridgecrest (760) 375-8000.*

If your out-of-town visitors have an RV or just wish to camp close by, the Desert Empire Fairgrounds campground is convenient and well arranged. The campground is very popular when there is a special event at the fairgrounds. Both RV and tent sites are available, as are sewage disposal, bathrooms, showers, and a laundromat. Spaces may be rented by the day, week or month.

## North Along the Sierra Nevada

### *Nine-Mile Canyon*

*Sequoia National Forest, Cannell Meadow Ranger District, (760) 376-3781. No reservations required.* The Black Rock Ranger Station is located in the area.

| Name | Location | Spaces | Open |
|------|----------|--------|------|
| Kennedy Meadows | 28 miles west of California 395 via Nine-Mile Canyon Road | 30 sites for tents, RVs to 22' | All year |
| Fish Creek | 8 miles west of Kennedy Meadows | 40 sites for tents, RVs to 22' | June-Nov |
| Troy Meadow | 2 miles west of Fish Creek, 10 miles west of Kennedy Meadows | 10 sites for tents, 63 sites for tents or RVs to 22' | June-Nov |
| Horse Meadow | 38 miles north and east of Kernville via Sherman Pass and Cherry Hill Roads | 18 sites for tents, 15 sites for tents or RVs to 23' | June-Nov |

## *Fossil Falls Campground*

*Bureau of Land Management, Ridgecrest Office: (760) 384-5400.*

This campground is near the lip of the fascinating waterworn chasm known as Fossil Falls, reached by traveling 35 miles north of the intersection of California Highways 14 and 58, then three miles north of Little Lake.

Turn to the right (east) on Cinder Road, then after six-tenths of a mile, take the right (south) fork of the road; in two-tenths of a mile take the left (southeast) fork; the other fork is marked "Not a Through Road." After three-tenths of a mile, the road ends in a parking area.

The campground has 11 unimproved campsites, toilet facilities, and picnic tables, but no water. (See the "Sightseeing" section for further information.)

## Independence Area

*Inyo National Forest, Mount Whitney Ranger Station: (760) 876-6200. Reservations: (877) 444-6777.*

The Independence area is well known as the entry to the beautiful Kearsarge Pass area with its many sparkling high-Sierra lakes. Hikers along the John Muir Trail use these campgrounds as staging areas. A wilderness permit is required.

Reservations are not accepted for the county campground, which offers spaces on a first-come, first-served basis.

| Name | Location | Spaces | Open |
|------|----------|--------|------|
| Independence Creek County Campground | West from Independence on Market Street for half a mile | 25 sites for tents or RVs | All year |
| Grays Meadow | 5 1/2 miles west of Independence along Independence Creek | 52 sites for tents or RVs | April-Oct |
| Onion Valley | 14 miles west of Independence at the end of Onion Valley Road | 29 sites, tents only | June-Sept 14-day limit |

## Oak Creek Campground

*Inyo National Forest, Mount Whitney Ranger Station: (760) 876-6200. Reservations: (877) 444-6777.*

The lightly developed area along the north fork of Oak Creek is directly west of old Fort Independence, with supplies and facilities available in Independence. The area is a gateway to Baxter Pass in the John Muir Wilderness Area. The campground offers a jumping-off spot for backpackers. To reach the campground, travel about two miles north of Independence on U.S. 395, then three miles west on Fish Hatchery Road. Stay on the right fork of the road, which follows the north fork of Oak Creek.

## Horseshoe Meadow Recreation Area

*Inyo National Forest, Mount Whitney Ranger Station: (760) 876-6200. Reservations: (877) 444-6777.*

Horseshoe Meadow offers a staging area for entrance into the John Muir Wilderness Area, the Golden Trout Wilderness Area, and Sequoia National Park. These camps are operated on a first-come, first-served basis, with a one-night limit at all camps except Road's End.

| Name | Location | Spaces | Open |
|------|----------|--------|------|
| Horseshoe Meadow Equestrian Camp | 3 miles south on Whitney Portal Road, 21 miles west on Horseshoe Meadow Road | 12 drive-in sites, equestrian sites | May-Oct |
| Cottonwood Lakes Backpacker Camp | Same, walk in from trailhead | 12 sites | May-Oct |
| Golden Trout Backpacker Camp | Same, walk in from trailhead | 18 sites | May-Oct |

## Whitney Portal Recreation Area

*Inyo National Forest, Mt. Whitney Ranger Station: (760) 876-6200. Reservations: (877) 444-6777.* Tuttle Creek Campground, run by the BLM, has no reservations and no fees. *Information about Tuttle Creek is at BLM Bishop Field Office: (760) 872-4881. Portagee Joe Campground* is a county park, with use offered on a first-come, first-served basis. *Inyo County Parks and Recreation Department: (760) 878-0272.*

Whitney Portal, the best known of the Sierra camping areas, is located directly west of Lone Pine with its county park, shopping facilities, and other services. The area is typified by the craggy, light gray Sierra peaks that surround Mount Whitney (elevation 14,495 feet), the highest peak in the contiguous United States. The mountain is about 100 miles from Badwater in Death Valley, which at 282 feet below sea level, is the lowest elevation in the Western Hemisphere.

The Whitney Portal campsites are jumping-off spots for an ascent of Mount Whitney along a 10.7-mile trail, an accessible hike for anyone in good physical condition. Between May and October everyone, even day hikers, must obtain permits. The hike has become so popular that the Forest Service has instituted daily quotas; you'd be wise to reserve your spot many months ahead.

| Name | Location | Spaces | Open |
|---|---|---|---|
| Portagee Joe County Park | 1 mile west of Lone Pine on Whitney Portal Road, just to south on Tuttle Creek Road | 15 sites, tents or RVs | March-Oct |
| Tuttle Creek | 3.5 miles west of Lone Pine on Whitney Portal Road, 1.5 miles south on Horseshoe Meadows Road | 84 sites, tents or RVs, 1 group site, picnic area | March-Oct |
| Lone Pine | 7 miles west of Lone Pine on Whitney Portal Road | 42 sites, tents RVs to 22', 1 group site | Apr-Oct |
| Whitney Portal | 13 miles west of Lone Pine on Whitney Portal Road | 44 sites, tents or RVs to 16' | May-Oct |
| Whitney Portal Group Camp | 13 miles west of Lone Pine on Whitney Portal Road | 3 group sites, tents only | May-Oct |
| Whitney Portal Trailhead | End of Whitney Portal Road, walk in | 10 tents | May-Oct 1-night limit |

Another campsite in the area is *Diaz Lake County Park*, 3 miles south of Lone Pine. *Reservations: Inyo County Parks and Recreation Department: (760) 876-5656.* Diaz Lake is a small body of water with a stunning view of the Sierras. Paragliders often soar overhead, taking advantage of the weather conditions. The Alabama Hills behind the lake have hosted many a Western movie. Fishing and waterskiing are both popular pastimes, with a 20-foot limit for boats. Diaz Lake has 200 sites for tents or RVs, with picnic tables, flush toilets, piped water, solar showers, and a boat ramp. Reservations are accepted, and the campground is open all year.

## Big Pine Creek Area

*Inyo National Forest, White Mountain Ranger Station: (760) 873-2500. Reservations: (877) 444-6777.*

Several campgrounds are located west of Big Pine, which has shopping facilities, motels, churches, and other services. The area features a deep, scenic canyon that serves as the gateway to the Palisades Glacier, the southernmost glacier in the United States. This area is a gateway to backpacking trips in the Sierra.

| Name | Location | Spaces | Open |
|------|----------|--------|------|
| Sage Flat | 8 miles west of Big Pine | 21 sites, tents or RVs | April-Nov |
| Upper Sage Flat | West of Sage Campground | 21 tents or RVs | April-Oct |
| Big Pine Creek | 10 miles west of Big Pine on road to Glacier Lodge | 30 tents or RVs to 22' | May-Oct |
| First Falls | Walk in one mile from Glacier Lodge road end | 5 tents | May-Oct |

## Ancient Bristlecone Pine Forest

*Inyo National Forest, White Mountain Ranger Station: (760) 873-2503. Reservations: (877) 444-6777; group camping reservations: (800) 280-2267.*

This area is located in the White Mountains northeast of Big Pine and north of the Westgard Pass highway. The world's oldest known living trees, the bristlecone pines, are here. The only water is at the old toll house on the Westgard Pass Highway, seven miles east of Big Pine.

The Grandview Campground, which has no reservations or fees, is a primitive camp (no water) on White Mountain Road, five miles north of Westgard Pass. Tents or RVs up to the 22-foot size may use the 26 sites available. Group campgrounds are in the Cedar Flat area, at a 7,200-foot elevation. Camping is available from May to November.

# South via California 14

## *Walker Pass Walk –In*

*Bureau of Land Management, Bakersfield Field Office: (661) 391-6000. No reservations, no fees.*

Located on the Pacific Coast Trail, the Walker Pass Walk-In Campground has two sites for tents or RVs and nine walk-in sites for tents only. The campground has water and pit toilets.

The availability of water in what is an otherwise arid area makes the campsite a favorite with people hiking the Pacific Crest Trail.

## *Lake Isabella Area*

*Sequoia National Forest, Greenhorn Ranger District: (760) 379-5646. Reservations: (877) 444-6777.*

Lake Isabella, a man-made lake, is located about 50 miles west of Ridgecrest on California 178 through Walker Pass. Camping supplies are available at Kernville, on the north side of the lake, and at Lake Isabella, on the southeast end of the lake below the dam.

The area offers fishing, swimming, waterskiing, sailing, river rafting, picnicking, bird watching, motorcycling, group campsites, and golf.

Campsites offer varied services including boat marinas and ramps, fire grills, flush toilets, showers, fish-cleaning stations, picnic tables, and RV hookups. Some facilities are wheelchair accessible and many allow pets if they are leashed.

The Kern River enters the lake at Kernville and exits at the dam. Both the lake and the river may become very dangerous very quickly. If bad weather approaches, leave the lake immediately. You should also avoid swimming in the river, which can be treacherous. In many spots, the river runs very fast, with a lot of hidden rocks and underwater obstacles.

The Kern River is known to offer one of the best river rafting experiences in California. Many of the rapids are rated Class IV and Class V and require a professional guide service. Parts of the river north of Kernville are rated too dangerous for rafting.

| Name | Location | Spaces | Open |
|------|----------|--------|------|
| Main Dam Campground | Southern end of Lake Isabella off California 155 | 82 sites for tents, trailers, RVs to 30' | May-Sept |
| Pioneer Point | West side of Lake Isabella, off California 155 | 78 sites for tents, trailers, RVs to 30' | All year |
| French Gulch Group Area | West side of Lake Isabella, off California 155 | 100 sites for tents or RVs, parking | All year |
| Hungry Gulch | West side of Lake Isabella, off California 155 | 78 sites for tents, trailers, RVs to 30' | April-Sept |
| Boulder Gulch | West side of Lake Isabella, off California 155 | 78 sites for tents, trailers, RVs to 45' | April-Sept |
| Tillie Creek | West side of Lake Isabella, off California 155 in Wofford Heights | 159 sites for tents, RVs to 27', 4 group sites | All year |
| Live Oak North and South | West side of Lake Isabella, off California 155 in Wofford Heights (family sites, 1 group site) | 157 sites, RVs to 30' | May-Sept |
| Paradise Cove | South shore of Lake Isabella, 6 miles east on Hwy. 178 | 58 sites for tents or RVs | All year |
| Camp No. 9 | East side of Lake Isabella off Sierra Way (primitive) | 109 tents or RVs, dump station | All year |

## Upper Kern River Area

*Sequoia National Forest, Cannell Meadow Ranger District: (760) 376–3781. Reservations: (877) 444-6777.*

| Name | Location | Spaces | Open |
|---|---|---|---|
| Headquarters Campground | 4 miles north of Kernville by the Kern River | 44 sites for tents or RVs to 22' | All year |
| Camp No. 3 | 5 miles north of Kernville by the Kern River | 52 sites for tents or RVs to 22' | May-Sept |
| Hospital Flat | 6 miles north of Kernville by the Kern River | 40 sites for tents or RVs to 22' | May-Sept |
| Gold Ledge | 10 miles north of Kernville by the Kern River | 37 sites for tents or RVs to 22' | April-Nov |
| Fairview | 16 miles north of Kernville by the Kern River | 55 sites for tents or RVs to 27' | May-Sept |
| Limestone | 19 miles north of Kernville by the Kern River | 12 sites for tents, 10 sites for tents or RVs to 22' | April-Nov |

## Lower Kern River Area

*Sequoia National Forest, Greenhorn District Ranger Station: (760) 379-5646. Reservations: (877) 444-6777.* No reservations or fees required for Alder Creek and Cedar Creek.

| Name | Location | Spaces | Open |
|---|---|---|---|
| Auxiliary Dam (overflow camp) | Lake Isabella, 1 mile NE of town on California 178 | Primitive sites, tents or RVs | All year |
| Alder Creek | 8 miles east of Glenville on Greenhorn Mt. Road | 12 sites for tents or RVs to 20' | May-Nov |
| Cedar Creek | 11 miles west of Wofford Heights on California 155 | 13 sites for tents, no RVs | May-Oct |
| Hobo #1 | 42 miles northeast of Bakersfield on old California 178 | 28 sites for tents, no trailers | All year 14-day limit |
| Hobo #2 | Same as Hobo #1 | 13 sites for tents, no trailers | Same as #1 |
| Shirley Meadows | 62 miles northeast of Bakersfield on Greenhorn Summit | 5 sites for tents, RVs to 22' | April-Nov |

## Red Rock Canyon Campground

*Mojave Desert Information Center: (661) 942-0662.*

A favorite camping destination near Ridgecrest is Red Rock Canyon State Park, which lures thousands of tourists each year to the beauty of its colorful rock formations. Campers at the park enjoy hiking, photography, stargazing, and relaxing in the magnificent surroundings.

The area is about 35 miles south of Ridgecrest on California 14. You can reach the campsites at Ricardo Camp via the old road that turns east from the main road. The park has 50 campsites, open all year, with heaviest use occurring from March through June and the end of September through November. Fees are charged for day and overnight use of camping and picnicking sites. Campsites are assigned on a first-come, first-served basis. There are no public phones and no group campsites.

The phone number above is located in Lancaster, but that office can communicate with the park if needed.

*Desert explorer in Panamint Valley* — *Linda Sappington*

# SAFETY TIPS FOR
# THE DESERT EXPLORER

The safety precautions summarized here are followed by all prudent desert travelers. Please review this section *before* you set out on your first real exploration.

Some of these tips may appear obvious and simplistic, but please remember that people are injured and die needlessly in our desert; both visitors and residents become lost, suffer from hypothermia, break limbs, get stuck, or become flash-flood victims.

The very majesty and beauty of our valley and its guardian mountains is caused by powerful environmental forces. Although the desert may appear flat and boring from the highway, a 15-minute bounce on a dirt road into a canyon will find you in territory that is unimaginably beautiful, yet confusing to navigate.

Simple precautions will allow you to explore fearlessly, find your own favorite desert beauty spots, and go home proud of your new skills.

The most common desert explorations may be grouped into three categories: *Civilized* (drive on paved, graded dirt, or gravel roads to a location where other people will be present; walk or hike for less than half a day), *Independent* (drive on ungraded dirt roads, select route for scenery and solitude, use local maps for navigation, make trip a maximum of one day), and *Adventurous* (make trip that lasts at least overnight, perhaps even a week or more; use climbing or other skills; take itinerary that includes "back-country" emphasis).

Each of these levels of exploration requires the same basic preparation. Also included are lists of additional recommended gear and preparations necessary for more ambitious trips.

# Basic Precautions

1. Check tire pressure and tread, including on the spare tire. Check fuel, oil, and water (include an extra jug of water for the radiator). Take enough water for twice your expected absence. A gallon of water per person per day is the minimum you should carry.

2. Bring maps and guides of the area, flashlight(s) with fresh batteries, sunglasses, sunscreen, hats, and warm sweaters or jackets.

3. If you plan to make several trips, create a kit to keep in the trunk or truck bed. Once assembled, the kit will last indefinitely.

Include such items as: tools (jack, tire inflator, duct tape, hammer, screwdrivers, wrenches, pliers, and electric tape), shovel, several old boards or carpet scraps for traction in case of sandy soil, compass, matches, lantern, pocket knife, first-aid kit, and first-aid manual.

4. Respect the weather. If you are exploring and notice a significant change in the weather, pay attention. Clouds, wind, and temperature changes may signal major changes in storm patterns.

Seek shelter during thunderstorms. Lightning is unpredictable, especially in the mountains. Be extremely cautious during rainstorms. Flash floods may accompany rainstorms, filling washes quickly with a powerful current, and gauging the depth of the water is often difficult. Stay on high ground until the storm passes.

5. Respect the river. Be extremely careful when wading, swimming, or boating in the Kern River. The swift current and many rocks make the Kern one of the nation's most deadly streams.

6. Carry appropriate gear. High-top boots aid in scrambling over rock and protect you from cacti and

(somewhat) from snakes. Remember that even when days are warm, nights may be very cold. Bring blankets, jackets, and extra jeans (wet blue jeans may speed hypothermia).

Better yet, invest in modern fabrics that work when wet and that dry quickly. Dressing in such fabrics is especially important in the mountains.

7. Familiarize yourself with desert rattlesnakes and with current medical advice for snakebite, which involves staying calm, immobilizing the affected part, and seeking immediate medical help.

## Precautions for Independent Travelers

For independent traveling, observe all of the above precautions, plus the following:

1. Take topographic maps. Outdoor supply stores, ranger stations, BLM offices, and book stores sell excellent topographical maps.

2. Respect the ground where you walk. Abandoned mine shafts and diggings may not be marked. Be especially careful to keep children away from mine openings.

Most critters will flee from you. You will see burrows and tracks of many animals. If an animal attacks and draws blood, return as quickly as is safe to Ridgecrest Regional Hospital for treatment.

3. Respect your intestinal tract. When you camp, always boil stream water. Use good sense in scavenging for wild nuts and berries. The best rule is to pack in your own food and only look at the interesting fungi and fruits near your campsite.

4. If you plan to go off-road or are beginning a hike or climb, make sure friends or relatives (or the local police) know where you are headed and when you expect to return. And don't forget to call them when you get back!

## Precautions for Adventurous Travelers

If you plan to travel off the beaten path, you need to observe all of the above, plus the following:

1. For an extended trip, take two vehicles if you can.

2. Consider joining a group, perhaps a commercial pack trip or hiking club event, for your journey.

3. Study the excellent guides to backcountry explorations for routes, techniques, and recommended equipment.

# SURVIVAL IN THE DESERT

One of the most frequent mishaps for the desert traveler is getting stuck in the sand. To avoid getting stuck, stay in established tracks; the sand is more compacted there.

If you leave the road, examine the surface beforehand. Allow enough distance between yourself and the car ahead so that you can develop sufficient momentum to clear sand traps. Know the clearance of your vehicle and remember that the clearance may be less if your vehicle is heavily loaded or if you have let air out of your tires.

Crossing washouts is sometimes hazardous. The wise traveler softens the contours of the edges of washes by digging or building them up with stones. Don't park in washes. At the end of the road, park your car so that a coasting start is possible if necessary.

Survival is a matter of staying calm, thinking clearly, and making adequate advance preparations. Above all, don't panic. If your car breaks down, or you become delayed for any other unexpected reason, consider your situation calmly. The temperature will allow you to move about safely any time during the winter months, and between sunset and sunrise during the summer months in the desert.

Wear clothing appropriate to avoid overexposure to sun: a long-sleeved shirt or blouse, sunglasses, and a broad-brimmed hat. In the winter, at night, the temperature can be expected to be as low as 20°F on the desert floor, so you will need warm clothing if you are forced to stay out overnight.

If you become stuck, exercise caution in rocking your car back and forth, since that may only mire you deeper in the sand. Bushes, stones, a piece of rug or a machinery belt may help you gain traction. As a last resort, letting air out of your vehicle's tires may increase the area supporting the weight of the car and thus provide more traction.

If you are only a short distance from a paved road where other travelers might be expected, you may decide to walk for help if you are sure of the distance and direction. Caution anyone staying with the vehicle to remain there, regardless of the delay involved in getting help. If the distance to help is excessive, it is best to stay with your car. A car is more easily seen by searchers than is a lone person.

If you can, rig a shelter on the shady side of the car from a blanket or other material. The temperature in the shade under such shelter can be 15 to 20 degrees cooler than in the sun on the first day, and, because of the insulating properties of the ground, as much as 30 degrees cooler on the second day. Staying cool cuts your body's water loss and reduces your water intake requirement.

You will have to do some rudimentary water rationing. Estimate the number of days you expect to be stranded (usually no more than two to four) and apportion water accordingly. The human body can subsist on little or no food for two or more weeks, but must have at least a quart of water a day, assuming a minimum amount of activity.

Drink your ration in larger amounts rather than sipping it; this gets the water faster to the tissues where it is needed and reduces losses caused by evaporation. Stick to your ration;

neither increase nor decrease it. People have died of thirst with water in their canteens.

Sources of water are available in the desert. Cacti store quantities of water. The barrel cactus is the most convenient for drinking water. The spiny outer surfaces of the cacti can be disarmed by burning off the spines. The cacti may then be sliced in two and hollowed out. Water will collect in the hollow and can be squeezed out of the fleshy material scraped from the hollow. The meaty portions can even be eaten in an emergency.

The general rule is to avoid plants having a bitter taste or a milky sap. Try a little of the plant or sap and wait eight hours. If you note no ill effects, repeat the procedure. After another eight hours, if you note no ill effects, it is probably safe for you to use the plant as a source of food.

Another source of water is from condensation. The desert sands are slightly damp below the dry surface layer. If you dig a hole about two feet deep and three feet across, water will condense on the under side of a piece of plastic spread over the hole. A rock in the center of the plastic and a cup beneath will collect the condensation. Certain types of plastic are better for this purpose than others; special survival kits may be purchased from ads in various western and desert magazines.

Stream beds will often have natural rock dams, behind which water will collect below the surface of what otherwise appears to be a dry wash. A hole appropriately placed will frequently fill with water in a few minutes.

The experienced desert traveler, when forced to depart from a prearranged plan or itinerary (such as having to use alternate routes because of washouts, etc.), will leave an indication of the route. An obvious arrow, with a simple message, a date, or perhaps simply your initials, will suffice.

# Survival in the Local Mountains

As mountain ranges go, the Sierra Nevada Range is relatively benign, but letting that lull you into complacency could set a deadly trap. Most days in the summer you can venture into the mountains with a T-shirt and shorts and survive. Sudden afternoon storms with wind and rain bring with them the ingredients for hypothermia or lightning strikes. The key is to stay dry and avoid the wind. Something as simple as carrying a large trash bag can save your life. The bag weighs almost nothing and you can use it for warmth in an emergency.

The China Lake Mountain Rescue Group holds a mountaineering class in early summer each year. This class introduces mountain travel and climbing. You can also find good books on these subjects in the Maturango Museum and local shops.

On your initial trips, a good idea is to go with someone familiar with the local mountains. Until you have experience, you should not attempt winter travel in the mountains.

Be aware that the Sierra peaks are high enough to cause many people to experience "mountain sickness." Though rarely fatal at local altitudes, altitude sickness can ruin your day as far as fun is concerned. Headaches, dizziness, and nausea are the most common symptoms. The cure is to move to lower elevations. Taking trips of increasing altitude will build a tolerance in most people. Many people fail to drink enough water, and the symptoms of dehydration at high altitude are similar to mountain sickness and just as unpleasant.

Remember that when you deal with nature, you can do everything right and still become a victim, for the mountains are inherently dangerous.

*Desert Primrose*

*– Mark Pahuta*

# Part Three
# THE NATURAL WORLD OF INDIAN WELLS VALLEY AND THE NORTHERN MOJAVE DESERT

*Taking only pictures, leaving only footprints*  — *Elizabeth Babcock*

# WILDFLOWERS

In springtime a multicolored carpet of wildflowers often covers our valley floor, with patches of color filling the surrounding canyons. A good spring display brings an influx of tourists, cameras and guidebooks in hand, to explore the roadsides, canyons, and washes.

Over the course of several weeks, flowers bloom on the valley floor, with later displays in the canyons of the nearby Sierra Nevada and Panamint ranges. Even in dry years when showier displays do not appear, beautiful little blossoms ("belly flowers") no larger than a child's fingernail may be found on the desert floor.

Contrary to popular opinion, springtime bursts of flowering do not necessarily correlate with the total annual rainfall. If a spectacular spring display is to occur, precipitation of well over an inch must come in late winter. Heavy rains in other months are not as effective. Even in dry years, a few flowers may be found in the canyons along the eastern slopes of the Sierra Nevada, notably in Indian Wells, Short, Nine-Mile, and Sand Canyons.

With the severe climatic conditions on the desert, plants have had to develop some interesting devices to survive. Many perennials have cut down evaporation by means of reduced surfaces (as in cacti); coverings of whitish materials, hairs, or thorns that may reflect light and avoid heat; or by resinous or mucilaginous (waxy) sap that protects the plant from water loss. Seeds of many annual plants have germination inhibitors that must be leached by a certain amount of rainfall before germination can occur.

A few of the more common wildflowers of the area are arranged here in family groups. We hope our short descriptions will help inspire you to learn more about our desert's fascinating plants. You can find excellent guidebooks in the Maturango Museum, the library, or any bookstore. The museum also sponsors a wildflower exhibit and wildflower walks each spring; call (760) 375-6900 for further details.

*LILY FAMILY. Well known as garden plants, lilies are generally showy perennials with basal leaves that have parallel veins. Symmetrical flowers in three or six parts grow from bulbs, rootstocks, or corms. Prominent desert members include the Joshua tree, wild onion, desert hyacinth, and mariposa lily.*

*JOSHUA TREE — White*

The Joshua tree has rigid, spine-tipped, dagger-shaped leaves. The plant is found on dry desert mesas and slopes at altitudes of 2,000 to 6,000 feet. In the spring, cone-like clusters of greenish-white, waxen flowers terminate the branches. Flowering is dependent on temperature and rainfall and doesn't occur every year. Woodrats, lizards, insects, and birds use the tree as a source of food, shelter, and nesting materials. Joshua trees may be seen in profusion as you ascend State 178 toward Walker Pass. March–May

*PARRY NOLINA — White to Cream*

Often confused with the yucca, the nolina has less rigid leaves coming from the base in a dense crown and the flowering stalk is three to six feet tall. White plumes several feet high are composed of tiny blossoms. This plant grows in dry, rocky places. Locally it is found in Short Canyon and on the South Fork of the Kern River. April–June

*DESERT HYACINTH — Blue to Lavender*

Common on plains and hillsides below 8,000 feet, the desert hyacinth or brodiaea has basal, grasslike leaves a foot or more long. A slender, naked flower stalk supports a small cluster of blue flowers. March–May

*DESERT MARIPOSA — Orange-Red Vermilion*

The desert mariposa is a striking orange-red with brownish-purple patches at the base of each of three petals. Generally a few inches to a foot tall, this flower may grow up through rocks and bushes. A flaming display of color can be seen some years on Black Mountain in the El Pasos. The color of this species varies with location and elevation. April–June

**CACAO FAMILY. *This family is a small one, with only three species in California. All members have alternate and simple leaves covered with short, soft hairs.***

*FREMONTIA — Yellow*

Named for Captain John Frémont, an early western explorer, Fremontia or flannel bush is a large shrub or small tree with a profusion of waxy yellow flowers about two inches in diameter. The name flannel bush comes from the feltlike surfaces on the undersides of the three-lobed leaves. This bush is found above 3,000-foot altitudes on dry, granitic slopes in canyons of the Sierra and locally in the Walker Pass area and Indian Wells Canyon. May–June

**CROWFOOT OR BUTTERCUP FAMILY.** *The members of this large and handsome family vary greatly in appearance. Some of the flowers have hoods and spurs; others have five regular petals with glands at the base. Delphinium, columbine, anemone, and ranunculus all belong to this family.*

*LARKSPUR* — Blue to Lavender

A lovely, delicate perennial, the larkspur has star-shaped flowers with a nectar-bearing spur that suggests the claw of a bird. Widely distributed on gravelly benches and washes below 7,500 feet. April–June

**MALLOW FAMILY.** *Most mallows are herbs with alternate, simple, and palmately veined leaves. The often showy flowers have five petals that are attached to a tube of united stamens. Cotton, okra, hibiscus, and hollyhock also belong to this family.*

*DESERT MALLOW* — Orange to Apricot

A shrubby perennial with palmately veined, grayish-green leaves, the apricot or desert mallow has showy, long-lasting blooms in a variety of colors. The plant is found along highways, on dry, rocky slopes, and in canyons below 8,000 feet. March–September

*DESERT FIVESPOT* — Lavender

A striking flower, the desert fivespot or Chinese lantern is an annual with round green or reddish-brown leaves. The rose-purple petals form a globe that barely opens enough to reveal five bright carmine spots. Its general habitat is in washes, mesas, and gullies east of Indian Wells Valley at elevations below 4,000 feet. March–May

**CALTROP FAMILY.** *A small family of herbs and shrubs with opposite, compound leaflets, the caltrops have five-petaled flowers and 10 distinct stamens.*

CREOSOTE BUSH — *Yellow*

The creosote bush is not only the tallest shrub on the valley floor (from three to 12 feet), but also the dominant plant over great areas of desert. Small, waxy yellow flowers cover the bush in the spring and later develop into fuzzy cottonseed balls. An evergreen, resinous plant, the creosote has a distinct odor, especially when it rains. Indians valued it for medicinal and antiseptic properties. The bush is the most successful plant on our desert. April–May (or later with rain)

PUNCTURE VINE — *Yellow*

The puncture vine, a prostrate weed that may spread to a three-foot radius, has tiny, pretty yellow blossoms that mature into spined nutlets. The nutlets are dangerous to bicycle tires, dogs, and bare feet, so when you find the weed, you should destroy it. Introduced from Europe, this pest is common along roadsides and in waste places below 5,000 feet. April–October

**LOASA FAMILY.** *This small family contains plants covered with rough, stiff hairs. The often showy flowers have four or five petals and numerous stamens.*

BLAZING STAR — *Yellow*

Blazing star is a name given to many species of the genus *Mentzelia*. Several in our area are annuals with five bright, shiny, yellow petals and many stamens. February–June

***GERANIUM FAMILY. Many species of the geranium family are well known as house and garden plants. All the flowers have five-clawed petals and five or 10 stamens. A distinctive feature is the fruit, a long-beaked, elastic capsule that coils when mature.***

*FILAREE — Rose Lavender*

The filaree is a small plant that has finely divided, fernlike leaves and tiny lavender flowers. It is easily recognized by its coiled, beaked seed pods. A native of Europe, this plant is common in California below 6,000 feet. February–May

***POPPY FAMILY. Poppies are annual or perennial herbs with milky or colored juice. The solitary and often showy flowers have four to 12 petals in two series. As the flower opens, the two or three sepals fall. The fruit is a many-seeded capsule.***

*CALIFORNIA POPPY — Orange*

One of the most widely known plants in the state, the California poppy can be either annual or perennial and varies according to location and moisture. Closely related species in the area include the desert gold poppy. The California poppy has a flat rim below each flower; this rim is quite conspicuous after the petals fall away. In the spring, canyons along the eastern slopes of the Sierra host a blaze of poppy orange. February–May

## PRICKLY POPPY — *White*

A well-armed, spiny, two-foot-tall perennial with lobed, grayish-green leaves, the prickly poppy has large white, crinkly, paper-thin flowers with yellow centers. When wounded, the stems ooze yellow-orange latex. Found in dry areas and along roadsides from 400 to 3,500 feet. April–May

*MUSTARD FAMILY, The large mustard family is characterized by herbs with pungent, watery juice and alternate leaves. Four-petaled flowers contain six stamens, the two outer ones short and the four inner ones long. This family includes cabbage, radish, broccoli, and wallflower.*

## PRINCE'S PLUME — *Yellow*

Prince's plume is a perennial with sage-green foliage and racemes of gold flowers reaching three to four feet tall. Outward-thrusting stamens and linear seed pods one to three inches long give the stalks a feathery appearance. A long-blooming plant, it grows primarily in selenium-bearing soils of desert washes and slopes from 1,000 to 5,000 feet. April–September

## DESERT CANDLE — *Purple to White*

A two- to four-foot annual, desert candle or squaw cabbage is usually unbranched with single stems and numerous leaves. Deep purple buds at the top of yellow inflated stems open into fringed white four-petaled flowers. Common on open flats below 5,000 feet, desert candles can be seen near California City and Randsburg and in the El Pasos after good winter rains. March–May

**BUCKWHEAT FAMILY.** *A widely distributed family of herbs, the buckwheats often have alternate simple leaves. Flowers are small and numerous. This family also includes rhubarb and dock.*

*DESERT TRUMPET* — *Yellow*

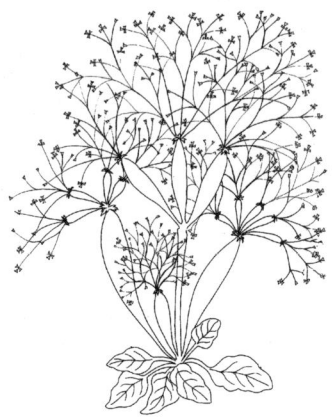

A two- or three-foot perennial with basal leaves and conspicuously inflated stems, the desert trumpet has very slender terminal branches with minute yellow flowers. It is common in gravelly and rocky places below 6,000 feet. March–July

*PUNCTURED BRACT* —*White*

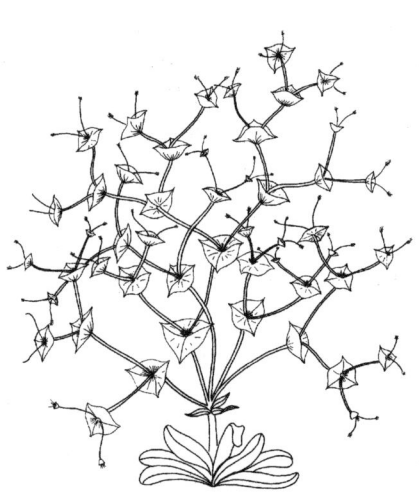

A short, spreading annual with minute flowers and horizontal branches up to a foot long, the punctured bract or saucer plant features fused bracts that constitute a series of saucers.

Stems pass through the centers of the bracts. With age, the bracts darken and dry to a brownish-red. Found in sandy and gravelly places from 2,400 to 6,000 feet. April–July

**CACTUS FAMILY.** *Plants in this family have developed many adaptations to survive in the desert. Cacti have leafless, well-developed, jointed stems that are often rounded, cylindrical, or flattened. The stems bear sharp bristles or spines and often have showy flowers that open in midmorning and close before sundown.*

*CHOLLA — Yellow to Green*

The branched, cylindrical, jointed stems of the cholla are covered with long, straw-colored spines that easily attach themselves to jeans, shoes, and fingers. In the spring, large yellow-green flowers adorn the plant. This type of cactus is widespread and boasts many species. April–May

*BEAVERTAIL CACTUS — Magenta*

Low and spreading with wide, flat joints four to 12 inches long, the beavertail cactus has bluish-green stems with no spines. Instead, yellowish-brown, sharp barbed bristles are set in depressions. Very showy, three-inch-wide magenta flowers cluster at the upper edges of the joints. The cactus is frequently found on dry benches and alluvial fans below 6,000 feet. March–June

**PIGWEED OR GOOSEFOOT FAMILY.** *Pigweeds are generally annual or perennial halophytic herbs or shrubs with alternate, simple leaves. The small greenish flowers have no petals, only a calyx of one to five sepals. Saltbush, beets, and spinach are also in this family.*

*DESERT HOLLY — Silver-Green*

Low, compact, and silvery, desert holly has separate male and female plants. The female flower has no petals, with its pistil borne between a pair of greenish bracts. Male plants host clusters of dense reddish flowers. The holly has vesicular hairs full of salty fluid that bursts out and covers the leaf with a gray shiny substance that tastes salty. Locally, desert holly is in danger of disappearing because it has been overpicked. It is found in dry alkaline places. January–April

*HOP SAGE — Rose-Purple*

Hop sage is a gray-green spinose shrub with separate male and female plants. The small leaves are gray-tipped. In late spring and summer, the shrub is covered with brilliant rose-purple fruits. Hop sage is a common forage plant on mesas and flats from 2,500 to 7,500 feet. March–June

*WINTER FAT — White*

An important forage plant, winter fat is an erect bush, two to three feet tall, with slender leaves. Fruiting bracts have spreading tufts of long silvery hairs giving the plant a white, woolly appearance. The "wool" is used by birds for nest linings. Winter fat is common on flats and mesas above 2,000 feet. March–June

*RUSSIAN THISTLE — Green to Red*

In spring, Russian thistle is green and fleshy. It is readily eaten by cattle. As it matures, the spine-tipped, scalelike leaves become sharp. When the thistle is ripe, it rounds up, breaks loose at the root, and whirls across the desert with the winds, scattering seeds as it goes. A native of Europe, Russian thistle is common only where soil has been disturbed by plowing, construction work, or vehicular activity. The plant has become an agricultural land-management problem. July–October

**FOUR O'CLOCK FAMILY. *This family includes many desert species of four o'clock and windmill.***

*SAND VERBENA — Lavender to Pink*

Sand verbena is a many-branched, hairy annual that has stout, trailing stems and small, fragrant flowers in circular clusters. This plant is common in low, sandy places below 3,000 feet. February–July

***PHLOX FAMILY.** A well -represented group in the desert, the phlox are both annual and perennial herbs or shrubs. The showy, five-petaled flowers are often tubular with five stamens. Of the several phlox genera found in Indian Wells Valley, Gilia is the largest.*

*DESERT CALICO — Pink*

This drought-resistant miniature plant has low-branched, tufted leaves an inch or so long with bristle-tipped teeth. The two-lipped flower is pink with a red-and-white pattern. Common in sandy gravelly flats below 5,000 feet, desert calico often occurs in dense aggregations on the valley floor. April–June

*DAVY GILIA — Violet to Pink*

Flowers with white-throated purple petals crown the delicate Davy gilia plant, which is one to two feet high. The stamens have a characteristic blue pollen. This gilia is variable and appears in a number of forms found in open fields and sandy flats from 2,500 to 4,000 feet. April–May

***BORAGE FAMILY.** Most borages are herbs covered with stiff hairs or bristles. The tiny, five-petaled tubular flowers are on coiled stems. Fruits are commonly four little nutlets.*

*AMSINCKIA or FIDDLENECK — Yellow*

Small yellow to orange flowers on a coiling stem covered with stiff hairs characterize the fiddleneck. These little white borages are forget-me-nots and are abundant. They are common in dry, sandy, and gravelly soil below 6,000 feet. March–June

***POTATO FAMILY. Members are chiefly herbaceous with the five flower petals united into a tube. Five stamens are attached to the wall of the floral tube. Many of the plants in this family contain poisonous alkaloids. Some of the potato family are important for drugs, others are valuable foods. Examples include tomatoes, tobacco, belladonna, and nightshade.***

*ANDERSON THORNBUSH — Light Lavender*

Anderson thornbush, a shrub with small, red, tomato-like fruit, is common on the desert and very noticeable in the spring.

*JIMSON WEED — White*

Jimson weed is a large, highly poisonous perennial with large, coarse, fuzzy leaves that have a rank odor. The large trumpet-shaped nocturnal flowers often have a violet tinge. Seed capsules are prickly. Jimson weed grows in open places and along roadsides below 4,000 feet all over California. April–October

***FIGWORT FAMILY. Members of this widely distributed family are mostly herbs or shrubs with tubular, two-lipped flowers. The snapdragon-like corolla generally contains four stamens. Fruits are usually capsules. Foxglove and snapdragon are included in this family.***

*INDIAN PAINTBRUSH — Scarlet*

A perennial with stems a foot or more high, Indian paintbrush has gorgeous red flowers that adds a bright splash of color to the desert in the spring. This plant is frequently found on dry brushy slopes from 2,000 to 7,000 feet in canyons on the eastern side of the Sierra and on the desert flats. April–August

## OWL'S CLOVER — *Purple*

The desert species is the showiest of the owl's clovers. Less than a foot tall, the deep red-purple spikes are composed of magenta flowers with lower lips of gold. Frequent on open flats from 2,000 to 3,000 feet. March–May

## BUSH MONKEY FLOWER — *Yellow to Orange*

This woody shrub has narrow, dark green leaves. The yellow to orange flowers closely resemble the snapdragon. Common on dry, rocky slopes from 3,000 to 7,500 feet. March–August

## WESTERN DESERT PENSTEMON — *Purple*

The tubular flowers of this narrow-leafed, herbaceous bush are violet with a reddish or purple cast. A densely bearded, sterile stamen can be seen inside the inflated floral throat. Penstemon is frequent in Walker Pass, Nine-Mile Canyon, and other areas on dry gravelly slopes from 3,500 to 5,000 feet. May–June

**WATERLEAF FAMILY. *Characteristic of this family is a five-petaled tubular flower with a distinctly two-part style. The flowers are on coiled stems that unfold as the flower blooms.***

## PHACELIA — *Blue, Pink, Lavender*

Several species of phacelia are represented in the Indian Wells Valley. The plants range in size from a few inches to two feet. Some have fernlike or divided leaves. All have glandular hairs that may cause a rash. March–June

*PURPLE MAT — Magenta to Purple*

Purple mat is a small, prostrate annual found on dry flats and slopes, a "belly flower." The size and number of the tubular purple flowers in any given season depend on the amount of moisture that year. April-May

**SUNFLOWER FAMILY.** *This family, the largest in the plant kingdom, includes about a tenth of all flowering-plant species. The flowers are often in dense heads, with each head appearing as a single flower but actually composed of many small flowers. The tubular, five-petaled flowers, called disks, contain four to five stamens. Long petals are ray flowers. The fruit develops into a seed. Desert members include tidy tips, pincushions, and alkali gold fields, as well as the flowers listed below and many more.*

*BURROBUSH — Yellow*

Burrobush is a low, grayish, globose shrub with finely divided leaves. Stem tips bear the heads of separate male and female flowers, the male consisting of small tubular flowers and the female possessing pistils surrounded by a burlike cluster of sharp spines. This is one of the more common plants of the desert, outnumbering the creosote bush at altitudes below 3,500 feet. February–June, September–November

*MOJAVE ASTER — Lavender*

Long-stemmed flower heads with yellow centers and 40 to 60 delicate blue-violet-lavender rays make this perennial a favorite of desert dwellers. The Mojave aster plant stands one to two feet high and has elongated, sharply toothed leaves. The yellow centers are disk flowers, and the lavender petals are ray flowers. Found in dry rocky places between 2,000 and 5,000 feet. March–May

*COREOPSIS — Yellow*

Coreopsis is a graceful annual, with each stem ending in a showy golden head one to three inches across. The leaves are two to three inches long. The plant features both ray and disk flowers. March–May

*DESERT DANDELION — Yellow*

As with the dandelion, the florets of the fragrant, pale yellow head of the desert dandelion are strap-shaped. The plant is a many-stemmed, smooth, hairless annual with leaves in linear lobes. Abundant in dry sandy plains and washes below 6,000 feet. March–June

*DESERT CHICORY — White*

The desert chicory is a weak-stemmed, two-foot-tall annual with layered, white-ray flowers with rose-purple veins on the outer side. The heads are large and fragrant. Common in the shade of shrubs and in canyons. February–May

*RABBITBRUSH — Yellow*

Rayless, narrow golden heads are borne in numerous clusters on the broomlike branches of the rabbitbrush, which grows to two to six feet in height. The stems and narrow leaves are often densely covered with feltlike green, gray, or white hair. A characteristic trait is the resinous odor. Rabbitbrush occurs in many forms and thrives on disturbed soils at altitudes of up to 9,000 feet in Eastern California. August–November

*CHEESE BUSH — White and Yellow*

This yellow-green shrub emits a cheesy odor when its resinous, narrow leaves are crushed. Separate male and female flowers adorn the same bush. When in full bloom, the clusters of female flowers surrounded by several silvery, membranous scales make a fine show. Cheese bush is widespread over the desert and dryer parts of the West in the alkaline soils of sandy washes and rocky uplands. March–June

*MINT FAMILY. With strong aromatic qualities, square stems, and opposite leaves, mints are an easily recognized group. The two-lipped flower is strikingly irregular. Peppermint, spearmint, thyme, and lavender all belong to the family.*

### THISTLE SAGE — Lavender

A basal rosette of spiny, woolly leaves forms an elegant pedestal for a stem that bears one to several dense, woolly whorls of lavender flowers. Orange-red anthers protruding from a fan-shaped, fringed corolla lobe make the thistle sage an exquisite plant. Common in sandy gravelly flats below 4,500 feet. March–June

### CHIA — Blue

A one- to two-foot-tall annual with basal leaves and a square stem, chia has whorls of tiny blue flowers. The seeds were used by Indians to make a refreshing drink and were roasted for food. Chia is common in dry and disturbed places below 4,000 feet. March–June

### PURPLE SALVIA — Blue-Purple

The purple salvia is a low, many-branched shrub with scaly leaves less than an inch long and covered with white down. Purplish or greenish bracts surrounding bright blue flower heads combine to make the whorled clusters quite striking. Salvia occurs in a number of forms on dry flats and slopes from 2,500 to 8,000 feet. May–July

### PAPER-BAG BUSH (BLADDER SAGE) — Brown and Purple

This shrub has greenish twigs and small green leaves. As the purple-tipped white flowers wilt, the brownish calyxes become inflated around them and develop into papery, bladderlike bags encompassing the fruit — hence the name paper-bag bush. The shrub is common in dry washes and canyons below 5,000 feet. March–June

**EVENING PRIMROSE FAMILY.** *Showy flowers with four petals characterize this family, which contains such species as fireweed, fuchsia, and the farewell-to-spring.*

*LARGE WHITE DESERT PRIMROSE — White*

Fragrant large flowers that open at dusk almost cover this low, short-stemmed hairy perennial. The one- to two-inch petals fade to pink the day after opening. Grows along highways, and on sandy slopes in Short Canyon. March–May

*BROWN-EYED PRIMROSE — White*

Stems arising from a basal rosette of dentate leaves host clusters of white flowers that are often reddish at the base. An annual, brown-eyed primrose is common on sandy plains and washes below 4,000 feet. March–May

**PEA FAMILY.** *This important family is composed of herbs, shrubs, and trees with alternate compound leaves. The flowers often resemble butterflies and when mature form legumes. Well-known members include mesquite, palo verde, lotus, clover, and alfalfa.*

*LUPINE — Blue to Purple*

Several kinds of lupine can be found in this region. Most are annual and have spikes of blue to purple pea-like flowers. The plants are characterized by palmately divided leaflets that originate from the leaf stalk at a common point. March–July

## LOCOWEED — *Reddish Purple*

Locoweed belongs to one of the largest and most complex of genera. This species is a poisonous perennial with inflated pods and hairy, pinnately compound leaves. The loose racemes are composed of small blue or purple flowers. Locoweed is common on the desert below 6,000 feet. April–June

## INDIGO BUSH — *Purple*

Indigo bush is sometimes as tall as six feet. The intricately branched shrub has grayish, pinnately compound leaves. Dark purple pea-like flowers have conspicuous glands on the calyces. One of the more common shrubs in the valley, it is distributed on dry washes from 2,500 to 4,000 feet. April–May

## DESERT CASSIA — *Yellow*

A many-branched, rounded shrub, desert cassia has numerous yellow-green stems that are leafless most of the year. The fragrant yellow flowers are quite regular, unlike the other pea family plants mentioned here. Desert cassia is common below 3,700 feet in sandy washes and open places. April–May

# Wildflower Tips

A visit to the desert in springtime will reward you with glimpses of many of the species listed above. With practice you will be able to spot wildflowers in unexpected places such as crevices in canyon walls or near damp spots left after an evening's rain. You may wish to start your own wildflower diary to track specific species or capture new examples. Consult the Maturango Museum for information on native plant organizations.

If you take the time to get out of your car and walk into the desert and canyons, you will see many miniature flowers you would otherwise miss. Even from your car, you can see

*Wildflower Show at the Maturango Museum, April 2001*
— *Elizabeth Babcock*

carpets of color, often made up of thousands of these tiny blooms. Please enjoy the flowers in their natural settings, but do not pick them. There are good reasons why picking desert wildflowers or plants is illegal. The desert ecosystem is far more fragile than it appears. Altitude and moisture changes that seem negligible to us make the difference between life and death to our native plants.

More opportunities for enjoying our native plants exist at the dozens of botanical gardens within range of a weekend trip — from Santa Barbara to Desert Hot Springs, from the Huntington Museum in San Marino to the Ethel M. Garden in Las Vegas. These gardens offer opportunities to view landscapes of flowers, succulents, and cacti and even purchase samples to try out at home.

*Snow Geese*                                    *— Elizabeth Babcock*

# BIRDS

The desert is rarely so silent that you cannot, by merely waiting a few minutes, hear the sound of a bird — and within the granite-rimmed margins of our valley, that voice may come from one of more than 300 feathered species.

Although some birds, like the tiny band of California towhees in the Argus Range, are sedentary and spend their lifetime within a half-mile of where they were hatched, many more are migrants that leave their birthplaces to travel, sometimes thousands of miles, to escape the threat of winter. Each October our community welcomes hundreds of snow geese that arrive to vacation for six months in the saltgrass marsh that borders the playa of China Lake. Each morning the geese fly in clamoring flocks to graze on pasturelands in Ridgecrest. They are a living connection to distant nesting grounds on the Arctic Circle, and to a distant time when ice-age waters flowed from the Sierra to Death Valley, making our valley a lush wintering ground.

Each winter, local Kerncrest Audubon Society members take the Christmas Bird Count, a census of all wild birds, residents and migrants alike, that can be found within a 15-mile circle centered in Ridgecrest. Migrant waterbirds drawn to the 200 acres of evaporation ponds at the local sewage plant comprise nearly half of the 80 to 90 species found at the site.

In spring different feathered visitors appear, many having spent our winter months in Central and South America. Among these are a dozen species of canary-sized, brightly colored warblers that actively pursue insects in our gardens. For a brief period in April and May, they and many others in a flood of northbound migrants swell the local bird population. Recent one-day spring counts have turned up 130 species in the valley and nearby canyons.

There is, in short, plenty of variety for desert bird-watchers, and the feathered population is always changing.

A bird book is indispensable for identifying visitors to your garden or new species encountered on your travels. Among the available guidebooks are *Western Birds* by Roger Tory Peterson, *Field Guide to the Birds of North America* published by the National Geographic Society; and *A Guide to the Field Identification of Birds of North America* by Chandler S. Robbins, Bertel Bruun, and Herbert S. Zimm. All feature color illustrations, with explanatory text and distribution maps.

For those interested in learning more about desert birds, the Kerncrest Audubon Society holds regular meetings and monthly field trips where the focus is on birds of the season. Members also participate in habitat improvement projects and local bird surveys. Information on activities may be obtained from the chapter secretary, P.O. Box 984, Ridgecrest, CA 93556.

Listed on the following page are some of the species of birds frequently seen in seven typical settings: *residential areas, open desert, stream-watered canyons, roadsides and farmlands*, and *wetlands*, with wetlands further divided into *marshes, shorelines*, and *open water*.

*Red-Tailed Hawk*                                        *— Griff Davies*

## Residential Areas
Cooper's hawk
Mourning dove
Anna's hummingbird
Costa's hummingbird
Red-shafted flicker
Pacific slope flycatcher
Western kingbird
Verdin
Ruby-crowned kinglet
Western robin
Mockingbird
Cedar waxwing
Starling
Yellow-rumped warbler
Dark-eyed junco
White-crowned sparrow
Brewer's blackbird
Bullock's oriole
House finch
Lesser goldfinch
English sparrow

## Open Desert
Prairie falcon
Burrowing owl
Lesser nighthawk
Horned lark
Roadrunner
Cactus wren
Say's phoebe
Le Conte's thrasher

## Canyons
Chukar
California quail
Great horned owl
Rock wren
Mountain bluebird

Western tanager
Lazuli bunting
California towhee

## Roads and Farms
Turkey vulture
Golden eagle
Red-tailed hawk
Kestrel
Loggerhead shrike
Raven
Western meadowlark
Cliff swallow

## Wetlands
*Marshes*
Pied-billed grebe
Snow goose
Harrier
Marsh wren
Red-winged blackbird

*Shorelines*
Great blue heron
Snowy egret
Killdeer
American avocet
Least sandpiper

*Open Water*
Eared grebe
Coot
White pelican
Canada goose
Mallard
Shoveler
Ruddy duck
Wilson's phalarope
California gull

In the following descriptions of some of our local birds, the numbers following species names give lengths in inches and, for some species, wingspreads in feet. The birds' seasonal status is indicated as follows: WV – Winter Visitor (typically October to March), M – Migrant (April–May, then September–October), SV – Summer Visitor (April–October), and R – Resident.

## GREBES: Thin-billed diving birds

### EARED GREBE — 12-14, WV

The autumnal movement of these inland waterbirds to seacoast wintering areas occurs largely at night. They seek open water for daytime stopovers. Local sewage plant evaporation lagoons lure hundreds of the sharp-billed, red-eyed transients. Their lobed feet, which provide swift propulsion under water, are set too far aft for easy walking. Each fall a few stranded migrants are found in town, where they have apparently mistaken parking lots for ponds and can't get airborne again. Returned to their element at the wastewater plant, they rejoin their kind in the fall journey to their Pacific wintering range.

### PIED-BILLED GREBE — 13, R

Marsh-bordered ponds often shelter a pair of these dumpy little divers with curious snaky profiles. In spring a vertical band of black divides their whitish, chicken-like bills. Often heard but unseen, pied-billed grebes proclaim territorial stakes with a loud *cook-cook-cow-cow-cow*. Downy young are garishly zebra-striped.

## PELICANS: Goose-sized fish-eaters with long, pouched bills

### AMERICAN WHITE PELICAN — 62, wingspread 8-9 feet, WV

Great flocks of huge white birds with black-tipped wings are seen circling on thermal air currents as they pass through the desert in April. These are white pelicans, the inland cousins of the coastal brown pelican, once on the verge of extinction from shell-thinning DDT. White pelicans nest on islands in the Great Salt Lake and a few similar sites in the Great Basin. Too buoyant to dive for fish as the oceanic species does, they appear on local ponds like a flotilla of becalmed galleons. After loafing for a few days they depart our fishless waters, heading north into Owens Valley or south to the Salton Sea.

### HERONS AND EGRETS: *Slender, long-legged marshland visitors*

#### GREAT BLUE HERON — 42-52, WV

Best known here for wintertime raids on goldfish ponds, the slate-gray, plumed great blue heron may stand four feet tall. Transient birds sometimes hang out at Lark Seep, a shallow cattail-fringed lagoon where they pursue frogs, mice, and the endangered Mojave chub.

#### GREAT EGRET — 38, M

Pure white with a stout yellow bill and black legs, the great egret is the largest of our egrets. This bird is often seen stalking along pond margins with its long neck outstretched as it pursues fish or invertebrates. When it rests, the neck is drawn back in a hump. Flight is slow and buoyant, broad wings beating a leisurely pace, long legs trailing stiffly behind.

#### SNOWY EGRET — 20-27, M

When the two common egrets are together, it is no problem to tell which is which. The smaller snowy comes only up to the shoulder of the great white. But seen by itself, the smaller bird must be identified by its slender black bill. In spring, breeding birds sport plumes that curve over their backs.

### DUCKS AND GEESE: *Aquatic birds with heavy bodies, thick bills, relatively short legs*

#### CANADA GOOSE — 35-43, WV

Occasional visits by big black-and-white "honkers" add variety to winter game birds that find refuge here. Canada geese will often graze on alfalfa fields, even golf course fairways, leaving wetlands to ducks. Their V-formation flights are not unique; white pelicans do the same.

## SNOW GOOSE — 25-30, WV

In October a flock of more than 800 snow-white geese, driven by ancient instinct, arrives from the Arctic to winter on the shore of China Lake, now a desert playa, but with marshlands persisting along its muddy alkaline shore. Here the pure white adults and their grayish offspring fatten on the roots of wiry saltgrass.

In recent years the flock has been drawn to the Burroughs High School fields and the city's irrigated pastureland near the fairgrounds, where the geese are protected and provide nearby residents a close-up opportunity to get acquainted with a species rare in desert settings.

## MALLARD — 20-28 R, WV

One of the most common of North American ducks, the handsome yellow-billed, green-headed mallard of city parks and country barnyards adapts even to desert life. In early summer, plain brown hens trail strings of ducklings hatched in the saltbush scrub that surrounds the wastewater ponds. By winter these natives are joined by arrivals from the north.

## GREEN-WINGED TEAL — 12-15, WV

What it lacks in size, the green-winged teal makes up in numbers; winter flocks of 300 to 400 are common. Dabbling for bottom food in shallow ponds, males show creamy-white flanks and dark sterns. Tipping upright they reveal bright green and cinnamon-brown heads. Females are speckled brown.

## SHOVELER — 17-21, WV

Wintering flocks of ducks usually include considerable numbers of these spoon-billed surface feeders. Males stand out as a contrast of black head, white breast, and russet flanks. When they preen on the water, they may turn belly-up and show bright orange feet. Females are coarsely mottled brown.

## PINTAIL — 13-16, WV

Handsomest of all the commonly seen ducks is the pintail duck or hunter's "sprig," its long neck and thin, tapering tail feathers making an unmistakable profile in flight or on the water. The dark head of the male is set off by white on the neck, curving into a crescent in back of the eye. Earliest fall arrivals are in nondescript plumage, from which they molt into the distinctive winter pattern.

## RUDDY DUCK — 13-16, WV

The ruddy duck can nearly always be found on isolated desert ponds, and here in late spring you can see newly hatched ducklings bobbing behind their mothers. At this time, males put on a spectacular plumage: black crown, white cheeks, cinnamon back, and bright blue bill. Wintering birds turn gray but retain faded white cheek patches.

***AMERICAN VULTURES:** Large, bareheaded scavengers seen in migrant flocks*

## TURKEY VULTURE, BUZZARD — 27-30, wingspread 5-6 feet, SV

To proclaim the arrival of spring, Capistrano has its swallows; Indian Wells Valley has its turkey vultures. Wheeling ominously over treetops in evening, they settle clumsily on branches or TV antennas for the night. Black turkey-like necks and featherless red heads are certain identification at close range. Soaring, they show light silvery wing patches against otherwise black silhouettes.

***HAWKS AND EAGLES:** Large soaring birds of prey or scavengers*

## COOPER'S HAWK — 14-20, WV

Those who maintain bird feeders in winter can expect to see this lightning-fast predator tearing into their sparrows. Cooper's hawk is an accipiter, with short, broad wings and a long tail to permit rapid maneuvers through trees and brushy cover as it pursues the smaller birds. Both sexes have a dark crown, a finely brown-barred breast, and a banded tail, but the female — as in most hawks — is a third larger than her mate.

*NORTHERN HARRIER — 18-24, R*

This owl-faced raptor patrols low above the marshlands in pursuit of rodents, small birds, or even grasshoppers. Males are gray and the larger females are brown, but both show a broad patch of white above the tail. Observations of breeding behavior suggest that harriers nest in fields of saltgrass and sedge near the China Lake wastewater facility.

*RED-TAILED HAWK — 19-25, wingspread 4-4.5 feet, R*

The husky figure of a flying red-tail, with its broad wings and tail, marks it as one of the *buteos* or buzzard hawks. A glimpse of the dun-red tailfeathers suffices to identify it. Light underparts are contrasted with a dark back, except in dark-phase (melanistic) birds sometimes seen here.

*GOLDEN EAGLE — 34-38, wingspread 6.7-7.5 feet, R*

Nearby canyon cliffs still afford nest sites for the majestic golden eagle, but its future is unsure. Fearless of other creatures, it makes an easy target for riflemen unaware of its protected legal status. Only the California condor is larger, and both species require hunting territory measured in square miles. The gold color is apparent as a sheen on head and shoulders when observed in bright sunlight.

 **FALCONS: *Swift-winged predators***

*KESTREL — 9-12, R*

This colorful falcon, smallest and most common of the desert hawks, often appears on fenceposts and power lines. The male's long, tapering, bluish-gray wings contrast with a red-brown back;

females are plain brown with cross-banded backs. The side of the head is marked with two vertical black stripes. The kestrel's typical raptor bill is short and hooked. The name, of old English origin, derives from the bird's high-pitched, crackling call.

*PRAIRIE FALCON — 17-19, R*

This desert species is pale brown and has a single vertical eye-mark. In flight this hawk can be recognized by a dark patch where the wing joins the body. Hunting from high poles, trees, or cliffs, it dives with swift wingstrokes to pursue small birds or rodents on the ground.

### PARTRIDGES AND QUAILS: Small, ground-dwelling, chicken-like birds

*CHUKAR — 12-14, R*

An import from the Himalayas, this game bird has found a new home in California deserts and arid parts of the coast ranges. State game biologists established this species elsewhere using hardy "natives" trapped here. Half again as big as desert quail, the chukar shows distinctive barring on flanks, a black V at the throat, and a striking red bill.

*CALIFORNIA QUAIL — 10-11, R*

Our State Bird is abundant in canyons and along the Sierra slope. Pioneers have appeared near outlying Ridgecrest homes, with the mountain quail found at higher elevations nearby. Both have plumed heads. The California quail's comma-shaped plumes curve forward; the mountain quail's are long and point backward. Coloring is predominantly slate gray, with white bands on brown flanks and scalelike markings on the belly.

## RAILS AND COOTS: *Chicken-like marsh and water birds*

### COOT, MUDHEN — 14-16, R

Ubiquitous is the word for this marsh dweller. Although a clumsy and reluctant flyer, the coot somehow finds its way to every inland body of water. Coloring is sooty gray except for white on the chicken-like bill and on undertail feathers. When pursued to the water's edge, coots run on the water surface to gain enough speed for flight.

## PLOVERS: *Medium-sized, shorter-legged shorebirds.*

### KILLDEER — 9-11, R

Along margins of shallow ponds or even on wet lawns, the active kildeer are seen probing for food. Facing the observer they present a pattern of horizontal black and white stripes: two black stripes cross the white breast and one runs across the nose to the eye. In taking to the air, kildeer call a plaintive *kill-dee*.

## STILTS AND AVOCETS: *Tall, slender shorebirds with long bills, contrasting plumage*

### BLACK-NECKED STILT — 13-17, SV

Black above, white below, this red-legged wader probes for food in shallow water, using its long needlelike bill. A nesting stilt will rise into the air to challenge intruders with insistent warning calls like the barking of a small, ill-tempered dog. The nest is a shallow scrape on bare ground, and the downy young birds leave it as soon as they are hatched.

## *AMERICAN AVOCET — 16-20, R*

Avocets have found a place to raise families here in the alkaline marsh area that borders the China Lake ranges. At the height of the nesting season, flocks of the tall, long-legged bird set up a clamorous *kleek, kleek, kleek* in defiance of intruders. Bright cinnamon heads are set off by white underparts and black-and-white wings.

## *SANDPIPERS AND PHALAROPES: Small, slender, shoreline foragers often seen in flocks*

### *LEAST SANDPIPER — 6, M and WV*

Shorelines of local settling ponds and alkaline seeps usually abound with the busy forms of several varieties of sandpipers, often collectively referred to as "peep."

The least sandpiper, sparrow-sized and short-billed, is one of the commonest species. Legs are yellowish or green, unlike the black legs of the larger western sandpiper, which also sometimes appears here.

A flock startled into flight moves with remarkable coordination, flashing white bellies, then gray-brown backs, as the flock wheels and turns as if guided by an unseen hand.

### *WILSON'S PHALAROPE — 9, M*

A traveler from afar, this slender surface-feeding phalarope spends its winters on the Andean plateau, turning north to breed in the prairie lakes and marshes of northern U.S. and Canada. In fall, tens of thousands congregate on Mono Lake, fattening on brine shrimp for the long journey south. Here, small flocks are seen spinning like dervishes, their needlelike bills probing for invertebrate life in the roiling water.

Females, larger and more colorful than their mates, are marked with a dark stripe on the neck and head and a wash of cinnamon brown on the throat.

## GULLS AND TERNS: *Wading birds and shoreline feeders*

### *CALIFORNIA GULL — 20-23, M*

"Sea gulls" on the desert are sometimes a surprise to newcomers, but the California gull is in fact an inland species. One of its larger nesting grounds is on two islands in Mono Lake. This species is credited with saving Latter Day Saints in Utah from the grasshopper plague of 1848. Birds from the north appear in fall as mixed flocks of gray-brown youngsters and gray-mantled white adults.

## DOVES: *Chunky, small-headed seed-eaters*

### *MOURNING DOVE — 11-13, SV*

The numerous "Dove Springs" that appear on desert maps are all named for the swift-winged mourning dove, which flocks to watering places in the heat of summer. Low, mournful call notes inspired this dove's name. Passing overhead in whistling flight, mourning doves show swept-back wings and a long pointed tail edged with white. They nest extensively throughout the valley, in trees where available or on the ground if necessary.

## CUCKOOS AND ROADRUNNERS: *long-tailed birds with two toes forward, two aft*

### *ROADRUNNER —20-24, R*

From creosote bushes beside the road, this long-billed, chicken-like native dashes across the observer's path, then stands for a moment of insolent defiance before it trots off into cover.

*Roadrunner        — Historical Society*

The roadrunner's slender profile, ragged crest, and long tail are easy field marks. Food choices include lizards, snakes, and even small birds and their eggs.

### OWLS: Flat-faced, nocturnal predators

*GREAT HORNED OWL — 18-25, R*

To spot this largest of our owls, you need to know where it sleeps, since these nocturnal hunters are rarely abroad in daylight. Habit will bring a great horned owl back to the same roost in a tree or building for weeks, and the spot may be marked by an accumulation of "owl pellets," dry, fur-filled castings of indigestible material that the bird regurgitates after a meal of small rodents. The "horns" are merely tufts of feathers that lend a menacing appearance, but have no other apparent function.

*Long-Eared Owl — Griff Davies*

*LONG-EARED OWL — 13-16, R*

The long-eared owl looks like a smaller great horned owl, but with ear tufts closer together on its head. A large facial disc, barring on its chest and belly, and white tail feathers barred with dark brown make this owl species easy to identify. It may be found in wooded areas throughout the northern hemisphere and is common in local canyons. Small rodents are its favorite food.

## BARN OWL — 15-18, R

You can scarcely appreciate the effectiveness of a pair of barn owls as rodent control until you have seen their nest site. Owing to all owls' peculiar way of bolting live food whole, then regurgitating feltlike pellets of indigestible hair and bones, the nest area is always littered with readily identifiable remains of the creatures on which they feed. Comic white monkey-like faces and quizzical expressions characterize this species.

## BURROWING OWL — 9-10, R

The only owl that lives underground, the burrowing owl rears its young in holes appropriated from ground squirrels and rattlesnakes. Small but long-legged for an owl, it was once commonly seen in sandy locations where several might be observed at their burrow entrance. Habitat loss and human incursions on nesting grounds account for most of the owl population decline.

## GOATSUCKERS: *Wide-mouthed hunters of the evening sky*

### LESSER NIGHTHAWK — 8-9, SV

After sundown in summer, nighthawks patrol the areas around street lamps, pursuing moths on the wing and often stopping to rest on the warm pavement. At such times the nighthawks may startle unwary motorists as they fly up in the glare of headlights. Their thin, tapering wings show a band of white near the tip.

## SWIFTS: *Speedy, saber-winged aerialists*

### WHITE-THROATED SWIFT — 8, SV

In spring the cliffs of Red Rock Canyon come alive with the twinkling wings of white-throated swifts, birds whose existence is an aerial ballet. They feed on the wing, scooping up insects as they soar across the cliff face, then reversing course to continue the hunt. Meanwhile they call to each other with shrill, twittering notes on a descending scale. Abruptly a lone bird may disappear into a crevice, there to feed its young in a nest of feathers glued with saliva to the sandstone wall. Only a practiced eye can distinguish the white throat and flanks as the dark forms flash by.

## HUMMINGBIRDS: *Tiny nectar-feeders, males with iridescent gorgets*

### COSTA'S HUMMINGBIRD — 3-3.5, SV, *some R*

Male Costa's hummingbirds have glittering amethyst throat feathers that extend backward in narrow points. This hummer inhabits desert washes, willow-fringed canyons, and arid hillsides. Its tiny cup-shaped nest, decorated with lichens and lashed to a branch with spiderweb, holds two pea-sized white eggs. With the help of hummingbird feeders, some Costa's hummingbirds remain here in winter while others migrate to Mexico.

### ANNA'S HUMMINGBIRD — 3-4, R

Well known in Southern California, the robust Anna's hummingbird has adapted to the rigors of the high-desert winter and can be found at feeders all year. The male has a shiny rose-magenta helmet; plain greenish females are indistinguishable from native Costa's hummingbirds.

## WOODPECKERS: *Stout-billed insectivores that cling upright on tree-trunks*

### NORTHERN (RED-SHAFTED) FLICKER — 13-14, WV

Some winters bring large visitations by these big brown-backed woodpeckers. Their undulating flight reveals bright vermilion underwings and tail and a conspicuous white rump-patch. Unlike other woodpeckers, northern flickers often are seen on the ground. Hopping awkwardly about on short legs, they drill lawns and gardens for worms, grubs, and ants.

## RED-NAPED SAPSUCKER — 8-9, WV

Sapsuckers are woodpeckers with a curious habit: they feed on tree sap. A horizontal ring of closely spaced shallow holes on the trunk of an aleppo pine shows where the sapsucker has been at work. After chipping out a row of shallow wells in the live wood beneath the pine's bark, the bird returns to feed on the carbohydrate-rich sap and insects attracted to this natural flypaper. The male has a clownish black-and-white face with red on throat, crown, and nape.

## FLYCATCHERS: *Slim insect-eaters that forage on the wing*

## PACIFIC-SLOPE FLYCATCHER — 5, M

A large group of smallish, slim gray birds appears in gardens and woodlands during the spring migration season. Most belong to the Empidonax group of flycatchers, and few can be accurately identified at a casual glance. One more common here in May is the Pacific-slope flycatcher, usually recognized by its yellowish underparts and a pronounced almond-like, pale eye-ring. It perches on an exposed twig awaiting the passage of a flying insect, flits out on semitransparent wings to snap up the morsel, then returns to its vantage point. Its only sound is a thin, upward slurred *tseep*.

## WESTERN KINGBIRD — 8, SV

This handsome flycatcher announces its return in April with a series of predawn recitals scarcely calculated to win friends among late sleepers. The unvarying performance consists of the phrase *kit, kit, feedle-di-di*, repeated again and again, apparently in an effort to impress a potential mate. Later in the season families of the sulfur-bellied, white-throated adults and their nondescript offspring line the telephone wires.

## SAY'S PHOEBE — 7-8, R

All flycatchers feed on the wing, darting out from a perch to snatch some flying insect, often with an audible click of the bill. The buff-brown Say's phoebe seems equally at home in uninhabited desert and around residential areas. It was known as a miner's bird in early days when it nested in mine entrances. Its tail is black, underparts rusty.

## *LARKS: Plain-colored, ground-dwelling birds*

### *HORNED LARK — 7-8, WV and R*

Though a few horned larks nest in the valley, many more appear in winter to forage for seeds in the open desert and around cultivated fields. At close range they show contrasting black markings over the yellow of head and breast, black whisker-marks, and tufts of black feathers on the crown. In flight, flocks utter a variety of high-pitched notes.

## *SWALLOWS: Airborne insect-eaters*

### *CLIFF SWALLOW — 5-6, M*

The swallows of San Juan Capistrano endeared themselves to the early padres by returning to nest at the mission on St. Joseph's Day each March. The cliff swallow appears here even earlier, passing through on its way to nesting locations in the Sierra and farther north. Travelers can see whole colonies of gourd-shaped mud nests on the undersides of bridges crossing Interstate 5 west of Bakersfield.

## *RAVENS AND JAYS: Stout-billed, heavy-bodied omnivores*

### *COMMON RAVEN — 21-16, R*

Nature's system of adaptive coloring seems all wrong for the common raven's case because this solid black bird is one of the few that brave the summer heat here. Birdwatchers familiar with the crow will note the raven's greater size, heavier bill, and deeper voice. Ravens enjoy aerial acrobatics, rolling, tumbling, and even passing sticks from one flier to another.

## PIÑON JAY — 10-12, R

Along desert foothills where Joshua trees merge with piñons and junipers, you can often hear the raucous, mewing sounds of a roving band of slaty blue crow-like piñon jays. Pine nuts are a dietary staple in fall, but in winter flocks may forage in cultivated fields.

### VERDINS: Desert cousins of the chickadee

## VERDIN — 4-4.25, R

The mesquite thickets of the Colorado Desert have given way to lettuce farms, and the verdins that once lived within the mesquite's thorny cover have moved north in search of suitable habitat. They have found it in Ridgecrest. The greenish desert cousin of the chickadee, capped with yellow and wearing a patch of chestnut on the bend of its wing, is a regular in local gardens. The verdin nests in trees or shrubs, fashioning a spherical structure of twigs, then lining it with plant fibers and finally a warm layer of feathers. All year long the verdin calls a solitary *tsee-ip*, as it goes about its pursuit of insects.

### WRENS: Usually small, slender-billed, short-tailed insect eaters

## MARSH WREN — 4.5-5.5, R

More often heard than seen, the marsh wren keeps itself hidden in cattail thickets while revealing its presence with a repetitious *tchuk, tchuk* and a remarkable springtime repertoire of reedy, bubbling notes ending in a low rattle. Patient observation may yield a brief view of the singer as it rises to perch on a tule stem. Its brown back is striped lengthwise with white, and one white line extends over the eye. Its tail is short and generally cocked over its back.

## CACTUS WREN — 8-9, R

Every sizable stand of cholla has nests of both house finches and cactus wrens. The bulkier oven-shaped structures belong to the latter, the largest of the wrens. The bird's slim profile, its rich brown head marked by white eye-stripes, and its prominently speckled white underparts provide sure fieldmarks. In spring the loud, ratcheting call of the cactus wren can be heard in Joshua tree groves where the species also nests.

*ROCK WREN — 5-6, R*

The distinct two-syllable call of the rock wren — *tee-you* — echoes across granite-walled desert canyons. Even when the singer is found close by, bobbing up and down on a rocky outcrop, no conspicuous markings are evident on the pale tawny plumage. Only when the bird takes flight are whitish patches on the margins of its tail visible.

**KINGLETS: *Tiny, energetic insect hunters***

*RUBY-CROWNED KINGLET — 4-4.5, WV*

As fall warblers depart, their place in the garden is taken by the active little ruby-crowns. They pursue insects from branch to branch, constantly flitting white-barred wings. On rare occasions the scarlet patch of crown feathers is raised, possibly in defiance of other kinglets. The white eye-ring is a dependable fieldmark.

**THRUSHES AND BLUEBIRDS: *Slender-billed songbirds***

*WESTERN ROBIN — 10-11,WV*

Whereas eastern robins are harbingers of spring, western robins arrive here in winter when hunger drives wandering flocks to forage in the desert. Around homes, pyracantha berries are a special attraction, and well-laden bushes may be stripped in a few days.

The robin's brick-red plumage is dulled in winter, and aside from an unmusical *tsee* uttered in flight, the bird is nearly voiceless.

## WESTERN BLUEBIRD — 6-7, R

In the canyons along the foot of the Sierra, western bluebirds have been found nesting in abandoned woodpecker holes. Unfortunately, they have sometimes been dispossessed by starlings, a new threat to our cavity-nesting native species. The male western bluebird, deep azure on head, back, and tail, shows a deep chestnut breast and nearly white belly. The wing is not barred with white, as is that of the lazuli bunting, which shares the same habitat.

## THRASHERS AND MOCKINGBIRDS: Long-tailed, slender songsters

### LE CONTE'S THRASHER — 10-11, R

The Le Conte's thrasher, a slender brown cousin to the mockingbird is at home on the broad, creosote-covered expanse of the high desert. The thrasher's song, heard as early as February, is a subdued rendering of mockingbird-like phrases, performed from the vantage of a cholla cactus or Joshua tree. This sickle-billed thrasher is the palest of the thrasher family; only its dusky tail gives any contrast to its overall ashen-brown plumage. Listen for a single whistled note, like a man calling his dog.

### WESTERN MOCKINGBIRD — 9.5-10.5, R

Locally, this hardy species appears to be extending its range along with human development. Scarce in earlier years, the western mockingbird now has resident status, nesting in shrubs around homes. Its virtuosity as a mimic of other bird songs is legendary. In flight its slender, gray form is accented by large white wing patches and a white-edged tail.

## WAXWINGS: Sleek-plumaged, crested berry eaters

### CEDAR WAXWING — 6.5-7.5, M, WV

A flock of these crested, snuff-colored migrants might go unnoticed in a leafless tree, except for their sibilant, high-pitched call notes. Silken plumage is accented by waxy red wingtips and by yellow-tipped tailfeathers. A narrow black stripe masks the eyes. Diet includes mulberries in spring, pyracantha fruit in winter.

### SHRIKES: *Small predatory songbirds*

*LOGGERHEAD SHRIKE — 8-10, R*

The "butcherbird" is so-called from its habit of impaling large insects, lizards, and even small birds on thorns or barbed wire. The loggerhead shrike can be identified by a broad black mask across the eyes and white wing patches that show in flight. Individuals are often seen perched alone on fenceposts or wires by the roadside.

### STARLINGS: *Short-tailed, sharp-billed, blackbird-like species*

*EUROPEAN STARLING — 7.5-8.5, R, WV*

After appearing as a winter visitor in the early 1950s, this unwelcome vagrant has gained a foothold in the west and is now an all-year resident. A medium-sized black bird, the starling can be distinguished from the Brewer's and red-winged blackbirds by its longer, sharper bill (which turns yellow in spring), shorter tail, and speckled salt-and-pepper plumage. Its call mixes high-pitched grating and whistling notes. It nests in holes in buildings or trees, displacing other cavity nesters.

### WOOD WARBLERS: *Small, bright-colored insect eaters*

*YELLOW-RUMPED (AUDUBON'S) WARBLER — 4.5-5.5, WV*

A momentary flash of yellow and gray, or a sharp, insistent *tsip* from a nearly leafless tree, proclaims the fall arrival of the most common of our two wintering warblers. Five conspicuous spots of yellow — under each wing and on throat, crown, and rump — provide identifying marks. In spring the gray is replaced by black breeding plumage as the birds move north.

## WILSON'S WARBLER — 4.2-4.5, M

When spring brings first reports of "wild canaries" in local gardens, suspect the Wilson's warbler, a brilliant yellow, hyperactive insect eater. The birds arrive in April on the crest of a migration wave that includes a dozen warbler species, which have wintered in Central America and Mexico. Most share a black, white, and yellow color scheme and have small, thin bills that mark them as insect eaters. A male Wilson's warbler has a velvety black cap; a female is a uniform olive-yellow.

## TANAGERS: *Heavy-billed, short-bodied birds, often brilliantly colored*

## WESTERN TANAGER — 6.2-7, M

Even couch-bound townsfolk who wouldn't forsake their videos to look at a wild bird are astonished by these gaudily colored transients. Bright yellow males have strawberry-red heads, black wings crossed by white bars, and black tails. Drab females wear olive tones. Tanagers may also be found on their summer nesting grounds in pine forests of the Sierra.

## GROSBEAKS AND BUNTINGS: *Colorful seed-eating migrants larger than sparrows*

## BLACK-HEADED GROSBEAK — 6.5-7.7, M

When mulberries ripen in May, count on hearing the melodious caroling of black-headed grosbeaks come to enjoy the feast. The male is black-hooded above a rusty chest and back and a white belly. As it flies, large patches of white show in wings and tail. Females are a creamy buff and lack the dark hood, showing instead light head stripes and a dark earpatch.

## LAZULI BUNTING — 5-5.5, SV

Lapis lazuli is a sky-blue mineral found in ancient jewelry. The lazuli bunting is a jewel of a bird, its azure head and back set off by cinnamon breast and pure white underparts. It nests in nearby canyons where its melodious warbling is a familiar spring sound. Females are a subdued buff-brown, with white-barred wings showing a trace of blue.

### TOWHEES AND SPARROWS: *Large family of plain, ground-dwelling species*

### CALIFORNIA TOWHEE — *8-10, R*

The plainest of brown birds, our California towhee is also a sedentary stay-at-home that spends its entire life within a short stretch of willow-shaded canyon bottom. Its call, a short, metallic *chink,* may be the only clue to its presence until the performer is spotted atop a low bush. Its undertail coverts are rusty brown, its throat marked with narrow dusky streaks.

### SAGE SPARROW — *5-6, R*

Broad plains of creosote bush and rabbitbush are the chosen habitat of the shy, pale brown sage sparrow. It lacks striking identification marks, with a single central breast spot and fine dark whisker marks visible only at close range. Still it is easy to recognize because of its characteristic way of running, tail held high, from the shelter of one bush to another.

### DARK-EYED JUNCO — *5-6, WV*

Another winter visitor recognizable from summer acquaintance in the Sierra is this black-hooded, white-billed junco. Small flocks mix with sparrows, gleaning food on the ground around bird feeders. As juncos fly, they show white outer tail feathers. Wings and back are brown, breast white. Of three junco races known in the U.S., our birds belong to the Oregon race.

### WHITE-CROWNED SPARROW — *5.7-6.7, WV*

Even on winter's coldest days the weedy margins of fields and roadsides come alive with the cheery three-part song of this traveler from the north. Adults brightly marked with black and white head stripes can be found atop nearly every bush, while dull brown youngsters forage below.

## BLACKBIRDS AND ORIOLES: *Stout-billed, medium-sized omnivores*

### RED-WINGED BLACKBIRD — 7-9, R

Perhaps the most abundant North American bird, the red-winged blackbird is easily recognized by the male's flaming red epaulets. Its mate is plain brown, faintly striped on head and breast in a pattern that provides effective camouflage in the cattail marshes these birds prefer for nesting. Such reed-grown areas are enlivened in spring by the male's gurgling *ook-ah-lee* call.

### WESTERN MEADOWLARK — 8-10, R

This meadowlark has a chunky profile, long bill, and short, white-edged tail. The meadowlark's mottled brown back affords good concealment in weedy places, but when the bird faces the viewer, it shows a butter-yellow breast marked by a dark brown V.

### NORTHERN (BULLOCK'S) ORIOLE — 7-8, SV

Experts have decreed that our Bullock's oriole and its eastern counterpart, the Baltimore oriole, are one species. Our bird shows a bright orange belly and cheeks, black back and crown, and patches of white on black wings. In town we also see orange-headed hooded orioles, particularly around tall palms in which they nest. No one will confuse their voices. The Bullock's oriole is a melodious singer; the hooded oriole has only a few harsh call notes. A third species, Scott's oriole, lemon-yellow and black, prefers Joshua tree groves.

### BREWER'S BLACKBIRD — 8-10, R

Once listed with the eastern Baltimore oriole as a single species, the Brewer's blackbird is now considered a distinct western bird. This blackbird forages in High Sierra meadows in summer. The male has pale yellow eyes and glossy black

 plumage with green and purplish highlights; the female is a uniform brownish gray. By fall, mixed flocks of these and red-wings frequent residential areas and nearby farms.

## OLD WORLD FINCHES: *Small, thick-billed seed eaters*

### HOUSE FINCH — 5-6, R

The most common member of this big family, the house finch is at home in the dooryard or the open desert. It nests on porch beams, cholla cactus, or Joshua trees, and makes it through the winter on seed from backyard feeders or roadside Russian thistle. The male sports a red head, vest, and rump, and its merry warbling song is heard from March into summer. The plain gray female is lightly striped on its head and breast.

### LESSER GOLDFINCH — 3.7-4.2, R

This diminutive green-backed cousin of the household canary is attracted by wild sunflowers or bloomed-out marigolds. It deftly plucks seeds from the ripening heads, scattering inedible hulls as it goes, and uttering a plaintive *tee-yee* as it takes flight. A bright yellow breast, black cap, and black wings with patches of white distinguish this goldfinch from two related species. Its nest is a tiny cup of plant fibers placed low in a tree or bush.

## OLD WORLD SPARROWS: *Early immigrants from Europe, now common in cities*

### HOUSE SPARROW — 4-5, R

This noisy, untidy species appears wherever man has settled. Its early spread from the east followed the railroads, a clue to its probable migration by cattlecar. If the house sparrow were not so common, it might be considered a handsome addition to the scene. The jaunty male shows a black bib, gray crown, and chestnut ear patches. Nests found in trees or under roof tiles are loose aggregations of grass and string.

*Coyote*                                    — *Griff Davies*

# WILDLIFE

Humans, creatures of the daylight hours, often perceive the desert as devoid of other life. While hiking a hillside trail or driving along a dirt road, you may be startled by a ground squirrel skittering from one bush to another or by a glimpse of a lean and tawny coyote. In the cool days of spring, when paved roads are the warmest place around, you may become aware that snakes live here, too, when you see a flattened reptile in the middle of the tarmac.

If you have patience and time to spare, you can easily spot many of the desert dwellers described in this chapter. Their signs are everywhere: burrows, droppings, and tracks reveal their presence and provide clues to their identities.

Most of our desert denizens are active at night. Many fur-bearing mammals and some reptiles find refuge from the heat of the day by hiding in caves and burrows or under rocks and bushes, or even by burying themselves in the sand. Lizards, despite being active during the day, are not partial to the heat. By moving from sun-warmed rocks to shady crevices, they are able to maintain their body temperatures safely below the threat of heat prostration.

Cooler morning and evening temperatures allow some animals to be out foraging, but they all vanish in the heat of midday. While the larger animals must visit water holes occasionally, many smaller desert species obtain their water rations from leafy food or as a product of metabolism.

The Maturango Museum in Ridgecrest and the California Living Museum (CALM) in Bakersfield provide excellent orientation for the amateur naturalist new to the California desert. Both feature instructive exhibits, and CALM offers an opportunity to observe live birds and animals up close, something rarely possible on the broad expanses of the Mojave.

## MAMMALS

### COYOTE

Probably the best-known large mammal of Indian Wells Valley, the coyote has a legendary history in the lore of Native Americans and early settlers. Although a coyote seen at the roadside may seem to the surprised observer to be larger than old Rover, the species is typically smaller and lighter (at a weight of approximately 20 to 30 pounds) than most dogs.

Coyotes are clever and opportunistic scavengers, and they eat anything — rodents, rabbits, carrion, and even household garbage. Unfortunately, coyotes are often blamed for predation actually done by free-roaming dogs. Coyotes whelp their pups in underground burrows in the spring, and may be seen in pairs at any time of year. On quiet evenings, the coyote's wild, high-pitched yipping is often heard in the outskirts of town.

### DESERT KIT FOX

Tiny and secretive, the desert kit fox is rarely seen abroad in the daylight, but may be spotted at night in the glare of headlights along desert roads. The little fox (adults weigh only three to six pounds) prefers the open areas beyond the city limits of high-desert communities. Almost completely nocturnal, the kit fox hunts rodents and insects. With its dense, sandy-colored fur, bushy tail, long slim legs, and huge ears, the kit fox is easily distinguished from dogs or coyote pups.

### BADGER

There is no mistaking the badger. Its broad, low-slung body, black-and-white striped face, and short but heavily clawed forepaws make it the most distinctive of desert mammals. It is an aggressive carnivore, using its claws to dig rodents or reptiles from their sandy burrows. Badgers are most active at night, but a pair may be encountered in the early morning prowling the rocky slopes in search of mice and ground squirrels. When pursued, a badger exploits its digging ability to escape underground.

*Bobcat kittens up a tree, China Lake administrative area*
*— U.S. Navy photo by Margie Hammett*

## BOBCAT

Although they are creatures of the canyons and mountainsides, bobcats are sometimes seen in the outskirts of valley towns where they come in search of food. Larger than any house cat, with stippled fur and short tail, the bobcat is readily distinguished from its domestic counterpart. Bobcats are solitary and largely nocturnal, preying on birds and rodents. The young, usually two to four in a litter, are reared in dens beneath rocks or fallen trees.

## BLACKTAIL JACKRABBIT

Lanky and lean, the blacktail jackrabbit is the classic hare of the desert. These jackrabbits are common throughout the Southwest, where their populations fluctuate markedly. Following years of better-than-average rainfall, jackrabbits appear in large numbers and many become casualties of highway traffic.

As with all hares, the young are born fully furred, with eyes and ears open. The doe prepares no nest, but conceals her young beneath a bush, returning frequently to care for them. Blacktail jackrabbits forage on a wide variety of desert vegetation and will visit gardens to sample cultivated plants. When pursued by coyotes or dogs, a jackrabbit's bounding pace can reach 30 to 35 miles per hour.

## DESERT COTTONTAIL

Smaller and more compact than the blacktail jackrabbit, the cottontail has much smaller ears, and is conspicuously marked by a snowy white tail. Young are born naked and blind in burrows dug by the doe. As with jackrabbits, cottontail populations swell when there is abundant vegetation, and the rabbits in turn become food for predatory mammals and birds of prey. The survival of red-tailed hawks and golden eagles is closely dependent on the reproductive success of creatures lower on the desert food chain, such as rabbits, mice, and squirrels.

## KANGAROO RAT

The Northern Mojave is home to several species of kangaroo rat; all are nocturnal and feed on seeds and leaves. They are often seen at night in the glare of automobile headlights, hopping across desert roads. Able to metabolize water from seeds and even bone-dry vegetation, they have no need to hunt for water holes. Deep, cool burrows are their daytime homes and sleeping quarters.

Kangaroo rats are named for their peculiar means of travel. They bound along like the kangaroo on strong hind legs, with their long tufted tails streaming back for balance. These rats have large eyes, tiny ears, and velvety cheek pouches in which they can carry prodigious quantities of seeds.

## DESERT WOODRAT (Pack Rat)

Secretive and nocturnal, the desert woodrat is rarely seen, but its large nest, a messy pile of sticks, cow chips, cactus joints, and man-made trash, is easily spotted beneath cliffs or fallen Joshua trees. The untidy architect of these homely accumulations is a beautiful little animal with huge brown eyes, luxuriant fur, a long furry tail, and big ears. Its largely vegetarian appetite runs to seeds, fruits, and cacti. Two to three pups are born per litter, with four or more litters per year. Desert archeologists have found fossil pollens in ancient pack rat nests that show the previous existence of trees no longer found at lower elevations.

## WHITETAIL ANTELOPE SQUIRREL

This hyperactive, racing-striped ground squirrel is familiar even to desert newcomers. Throughout the year it forages in broad daylight, dashing between creosote bushes as it searches for seeds, insects, and leaves. Like the kangaroo rat, the antelope squirrel does not need water, allowing the species to extend its range throughout the arid Southwest.

The squirrels live in burrows, where they raise one or two litters of six to 10 young each year. This little squirrel, sometimes misnamed a "chipmunk," is easily identified by its white tail, which is carried parasol-fashion over its back when it runs.

## BATS (various species)

Our desert is the preferred home of several species of bats, members of an exclusive family of flying mammals called Chiroptera — the "hand-wings." Some, like the Mexican freetail bat, are migratory visitors, appearing here from spring to autumn, but many bats also live here all year. Most, like the three-inch-long California myotis, are quite small, but there are a few larger species. The pallid bat reaches five and one-half inches.

All of our local bats are insectivorous and nocturnal, emerging from their daytime roosts in the evening to flitter erratically about in pursuit of flying insects. They locate their prey in the dark by listening for echoes of ultrasonic vocal signals.

## DESERT BIGHORN SHEEP

Increasingly rare and seen only in a few isolated desert ranges, the desert bighorn sheep is a magnificent animal prized by artists and photographers as a symbol of the Old West.

Rams and ewes both bear horns, those of the rams massive and so curved that in older animals the ends turn forward. The ewes' horns are short, slim, and only slightly curved. Males and females live separately in the summer, with the rams rejoining the ewes and lambs in the autumn rutting season. Lambs, single or rare twins, are born in the spring.

The herd, which may include a dozen animals, is usually led by an old ewe. The group will travel far from water, returning to springs or waterholes every few days. Death Valley National Park offers your best chance of seeing a desert bighorn, although the sheep are extremely wary and hesitate to drink if disturbed even by distant observers. The decline of this species has been linked to poaching, disease, habitat degradation, and competition from burros.

## BURRO

A native of the Eastern Mediterranean and North African regions, the burro earned its place in Western history as the companion of the lonely prospector. Today's wild burros are the descendants of animals abandoned by miners with the advent of the Model-T Ford.

Controversy surrounds the question of how much the burro's impact on its fragile desert environment was responsible for the decline of the bighorn sheep. For that reason, the burro has been both hunted and protected by law at different times. Today the burro and wild horse populations are controlled, with the animals enjoying protection under federal law. Following regular roundups by Bureau of Land

Management wranglers, healthy wild burros and horses are collected at the BLM Ridgecrest holding facility, then offered for adoption.

## REPTILES

### CHUCKWALLA

Our largest lizard, the sooty-colored, thick-bodied chuckwalla is a dweller of rocky hillsides, lava flows, and rock outcroppings. Like others lizards, the chuckwalla often basks on the rocks. When it is frightened, it dashes to safety in the nearest crevice. Here, by gulping air into its lungs, it wedges itself in so tightly that it cannot be removed without injury.

Despite the chuckwalla's fearsome appearance, the lizard is a harmless herbivore. Judging from droppings, a favorite food is the tender foliage of the creosote bush.

### COLLARED LIZARD

The handsome collared lizard has striking black and white neck bands, and many small spots and bands over the rest of the body. Adults are paler than youngsters, but the collar is always conspicuous. Collared lizards are carnivorous, eating insects and smaller lizards. They are agile climbers, excellent jumpers, and fast runners, often holding their forelimbs off the ground and their tails high. Young lizard collectors learn that the collared lizard can inflict a painful, though harmless, bite.

### LEOPARD LIZARD

Unlike its namesake, the leopard lizard *can* change its spots. The same specimen may show a light body with bold dark spots, then later display a dark body crossed by light bars, with the spots nearly invisible. During the spring breeding season, females have bright orange patches on their sides. Truly omnivorous, leopard lizards eat insects, other lizards, small mammals, seeds, and flowers. Like their close relatives the collared lizards, leopard lizards run bipedally when they are in a hurry. They are also ill-tempered and will bite the hand that attempts to hold them captive.

## DESERT HORNED LIZARD

Still called "horned toad" (even though it is not a toad and doesn't have real horns), this small lizard lives on alluvial fans, gravelly areas, sandy washes, and dune edges. It thrives in warm temperatures, which bring out an abundance of insects and ants, its favorite foods.

The mottled, spiky form of the desert horned lizard provides wonderful camouflage when it remains motionless on a gravel background, but the lizard is slow-moving and easily caught. For reasons still unclear, horned lizards in the Mojave are declining, and one species has been proposed for threatened status. Once frequently encountered, these charming little lizards are now uncommon.

## DESERT IGUANA

Like mad dogs and Englishmen, the desert iguana is often out and about in the noonday sun, especially in spring when it feeds on an abundance of succulent herbage. Larger specimens of the desert iguana are more than a foot long. The iguana is pale gray with brown bars and spots on the sides and a ridge of small scales running down the middle of its back. Desert iguanas are mainly herbivorous and can be found climbing in creosote bushes to reach the young leaves they seem to prefer.

## BANDED GECKO

On a dusty desert road at night, a pale, twiglike object appears in the headlights' glare, then moves a short distance and stops. Indeed it is no twig, but a small reptile in search of its supper. The banded gecko is a delicate-looking little lizard, with a pinkish or yellow translucent skin banded with brown. The gecko's scales, unlike a lizard's, are tiny and granular.

Nocturnal in habit, the gecko takes refuge during the day beneath rocks, logs, and backyard debris. It is lightning fast in pursuit of prey and uses adhesive pads on its feet to clamber up rock walls and even traverse the ceilings of miners' cabins. The gecko's diet is mainly small invertebrates, spiders, and insects. Collectors take note: rough handling will cause the banded gecko's fragile tail to break off.

## WESTERN WHIPTAIL

The western whiptail is a ground-hugging, long-tailed lizard that whips across open spaces with a sinuous, tail-twitching motion. The species is quite variable in color, but individuals are generally covered with dark spots and stripes on a background of brown, gray, or tan; the head-end is usually somewhat darker than the tail. Whiptails are active during the day, preferring the more open areas of the desert where they seek insects for food, often flicking their forked tongues in snakelike fashion.

## YUCCA NIGHT LIZARD

Once thought to be a rare desert species but now known for its secretive and nocturnal habits, the yucca night lizard lives in the rotting spines of fallen Joshua trees, or beneath dry forest debris and rock piles. An inconspicuous, finger-sized, small gray lizard camouflaged with fine black speckling, it eats insects, spiders, and other arthropods that share the dark recesses of its home. Yucca night lizards are viviparous; they do not lay eggs, but bear their (one to three) young alive.

## ZEBRA-TAILED LIZARD

The bold black-and-white striped tail is the major fieldmark of the zebra-tailed lizard; it also sports paired black stripes on the sides of its pale yellowish belly. The upper body color is a dusky brown, sometimes tinged bluish, and finely speckled overall with darker brown or black.

When pursued, the zebra-tailed lizard runs rapidly with its tail raised and curved over its back. If pressed, it may leave its tail twitching in the sand to decoy the would-be predator. This lizard's diet includes insects, spiders, other lizards, and occasionally plant materials.

## SIDE-BLOTCHED LIZARD

Small and quick, the side-blotched lizard is probably our most common reptile. It is named for the dark bluish or black areas on each side of its body behind the front legs. It eats insects, spiders, and other small invertebrates, and is itself preyed on by larger lizards, snakes, and birds. This lizard is active most of the year, and is found in a wide variety of habitats: desert scrub, canyons, rocky slopes, and around homes in rural areas.

## DESERT TORTOISE

California's official State Reptile, the desert tortoise is listed as a threatened species by both federal and state wildlife agencies. Tortoises are long-lived (more than 70 years) and remarkably adapted to the desert, but they are slow to reach maturity and particularly vulnerable to habitat encroachment. Great losses have been seen in the youngest age groups, and ravens have been implicated as predators on first-year animals. Only five of 100 baby tortoises will live to adulthood, and they will not reach sexual maturity for 15 to 20 years.

Desert tortoises escape summer heat and winter cold by digging burrows, sometimes 30 feet or more in length. An individual tortoise may have several burrows in its territory. Desert tortoises depend upon a wide variety of plants and range widely in search of food. Thus their lifestyle is adversely impacted by practically all human uses of the desert.

To overcome this problem, the Desert Tortoise Natural Area, a 40-square-mile preserve, has been established north of California City as part of the ongoing tortoise recovery program.

## COACHWHIP (Red Racer)

One of the region's most common snakes is the coachwhip, also called the red racer. Slim, graceful, and **very** fast, it is easily identified by the pinkish-tan body color, with black bands on the neck. The scales of the tail resemble the braided end of a whip.

The coachwhip tolerates higher temperatures than do some other desert snakes, and it can be seen out and about in very warm weather, hunting for small mammals, insects, birds, eggs, lizards, and even other snakes. The coachwhip is not venomous, but will almost always attempt to bite a person who catches it.

## RATTLESNAKES

Rattlesnakes are an integral part of the Mojave Desert ecosystem, where they play an important role in controlling the rodent population. They should not be killed capriciously. Several species are found in the Indian Wells Valley; all are venomous, but if left alone, they represent little threat to man.

Snakebite, though rare, should be taken seriously and medical treatment sought immediately. Prevention is naturally the best course. Be attentive when you're hiking — look where you put your hands and feet, and listen to the desert as you hike.

If you hear a rattler, hold still until you can locate it, then leave it alone. Use care in handling a road-killed rattler, since mangled and even seemingly dead rattlesnakes may still be able to bite careless hands. Rattlesnakes are not aggressive, and will strike only when they feel threatened. Don't tease or torment them. They will retreat to safety if allowed to escape.

## MOJAVE RATTLESNAKE

Often incorrectly called the "Mojave green," the Mojave rattlesnake may be reddish, gray, blackish, brown, and on occasion greenish-gray. The underbody is pale cream or gray, the back has well-defined diamond patterns, and the tail has black and white rings.

The Mojave rattlesnake usually subsists on small birds and mammals that it pursues both day and night, depending on the temperature. Like all rattlesnakes, it bears its young alive. This handsome snake, often thick as a man's wrist, is dangerous, as are all rattlesnakes of the upper Mojave Desert. The Mojave rattlesnake's venom has hemotoxin, neurotoxin, and cardiotoxin components.

Rapid heart rate, swelling, pain, nausea, vomiting, and respiratory collapse can occur after a rattlesnake bite. A bite requires immediate medical care. Do not waste valuable time trying to find or kill the snake. The antivenin now in use is not species-specific, so you do not need to identify the species of the offending snake.

## SIDEWINDER

The sidewinder is a fairly common rattlesnake of the open desert and sandy soil of the Indian Wells Valley. Named for its method of locomotion, the sidewinder travels sideways, the body moving in repeated parallel S curves. The tracks of a sidewinder resemble a series of Js, the curved hook indicating the forward direction of movement.

Adult sidewinders, scarcely more than two feet long, are small compared to their diamondback cousins. Their colors range from pale tan through pinkish or gray, with indistinct darker squares down the back. Small protruding scales above each eye give the snake a horned appearance. The sidewinder eats birds and mammals and bears its young alive. It is largely nocturnal.

## COMMON KING SNAKE

The common king snake is a handsome reptile, usually chocolate brown or black with a pattern of cream-colored rings over the length of the body. An occasional king snake may be almost entirely dark or may have a single stripe down its back.

The common king snake will devour other snakes, even rattlers, and rounds out its diet with small mammals, lizards, and birds. If threatened, king snakes may hiss, vibrate their tails, and even strike in a way that mimics the rattlesnake.

## GOPHER SNAKE

The gopher snake, heavy-bodied and often four feet long, is creamy or pinkish with brown or black patches down its back. These common snakes are sometimes mistaken for rattlesnakes since, like many snakes, they may shake the tips of their tails when they are frightened. The mimicry may include coiling and striking, even swelling the jaws to create the fearsome appearance of a rattlesnake, all of which are likely to bring the nonvenomous gopher snake to an untimely end.

Gopher snakes are both climbers and burrowers, pursuing rodents into their burrows and birds to their nests. The snakes kill their prey by constriction, then swallow it whole. They are found in most habitats: green desert, rocky hillsides, Sierra foothills, and outskirts of towns.

## ARACHNIDS

### SCORPION

One of the desert's most frightful-looking creatures, the scorpion faces its antagonist with a pair of menacing claws and a curling, stinger-tipped tail. Although some species can inject a potentially lethal toxin, the local species is not deadly. The poison secreted by a pair of glands at the base of the stinger may still cause a painful wound.

Reclusive by nature, a scorpion goes unseen until surprised in its hiding place beneath a rock, under a fallen log, or in a hiker's bedroll. At such times they are best allowed to depart unmolested, since they perform a useful service by feeding on harmful insects and spiders. The creature's pale yellow body fluoresces blue under the prospector's ultraviolet light.

Looking much more ferocious than it is, the desert hairy scorpion can be as large as five and one-half inches long from its claws to its stinger-tipped tail. Yet the sting is no more painful than that of a honey bee, and similarly is not life threatening unless the victim is acutely allergic to the venom. Scorpions are nocturnal hunters and use their sting to subdue the insects on which they prey. Females give birth to live young, and a mother may be seen with dozens of babies clinging to her back.

## SOLPUGID

The solpugid, a mild-mannered relative of the scorpion, has been called the most fearsome-looking creature in the desert. Though scarcely two inches long, when viewed with a magnifier its scorpion-like body is seen to be armed with a pair of menacing pincers. These are used to grasp and dissect insects and spiders, including black widows, that are then consumed with the aid of enzymes that liquefy the victim's flesh. Often seen near porch lights and on window screens in summer, the solpugid moves with astonishing speed in pursuit of insect prey. It is sometimes mistaken for the vinegaroon or whip scorpion, an unrelated Midwestern species.

## BLACK WIDOW SPIDER

The bite of the black widow spider, a glossy black resident of woodpiles and garages, is very painful, and may occasionally be fatal. Named for the cannibalistic habit of eating her mate, the black widow is usually secretive and not easily provoked. The mature female is jet black and is readily identified by a red to yellowish hourglass marking on the underside of her abdomen. The unfortunate male is much smaller and brown with light spots or stripes.

Black widows weave their tough, rather messy-looking webs in dark corners where they snare unwary moths, beetles, and crickets. A web may also support one or several round white egg cases, from which hundreds of spiderlings will eventually emerge.

## TARANTULA

Tarantulas are large, hairy spiders that live in the ground in burrows lined with silk. The tarantula does not spin a web, but swiftly overtakes its insect prey on foot. It feeds on grasshoppers and other large insects. In spring the males travel in search of mates, and during this season they are often encountered on desert roads. Tarantulas are timid animals, and very rarely bite humans. When they do, their venom has little effect.

## INSECTS AND OTHER ARTHROPODS

The upper Mojave region has many insects and other arthropods, the most numerous of nature's lesser creatures. A few deserve brief mention because of their roles in desert ecosystems.

Ants are common, particularly the seed-eating types such as harvester ants, whose mounds may be seen surrounded by chaff and hulls of seeds they have gathered and stored. Biologists have estimated that ants alone account for a third of the desert's animal biomass. They are preyed upon by ant lions, or "doodle bugs," that lie waiting in little pits in the sand to capture ants and other small insects.

Numerous moths may be seen around light sources or sipping nectar from flowers. The many species of sphinx moth larvae seen in garden foliage include hornworms that consume grape leaves and tomato plants.

Grasshoppers are abundant in the spring and summer. The chirping of crickets is an essential part of the summer insect chorus.

Desert butterflies include painted ladies, abundant in good wildflower years, and migrant monarchs that pass this way as they travel from wintering grounds in Mexico. The female Mutillid wasp is wingless; the male bears wings and is sometimes known as the velvet ant. Tarantula hawks, which are also wasps, have flame-colored wings and prey on the tarantula.

Soldier beetles, with their bright orange heads and dark purple wing covers, are seen in large numbers in some years. The small black darkling ground beetle is often seen. Blister beetles are also commonly found in this area. The praying mantis blends with the foliage where it waits, motionless, until some insect comes near enough to be caught.

Centipedes and millipedes are not common and are usually found only in the cooler months after rains.

Various species of bees can be seen pollinating the flowers. Mosquitoes have appeared in cultivated areas where water has been allowed to accumulate. Dragonflies and damselflies may be seen over a lawn at dusk, especially in parts of town that have standing water.

## FAIRY SHRIMP

No discussion of desert invertebrates would be complete without mention of the odd little shrimp that inhabit our usually dry lakes. During the summer, shallow ponds created by rainstorms may come alive with the nearly transparent crustaceans known as fairy shrimp.

The eggs may lie dormant in the dried mud of the playa for several years or more. With the appearance of sufficient water, they quickly hatch and mature. A new crop of eggs is then deposited to await the next deluge, which may occur many years later.

# Wildlife Identification — Terminology

Some of the desert dwellers mentioned in this chapter are listed below by both common and scientific names to aid in locating them in standard guidebooks:

| Common Name | Latin Name |
|---|---|
| Badger | *Taxidea taxus* |
| Banded gecko | *Coleonyx variegatus* |
| Blacktail jackrabbit | *Lepus californicus* |
| Bobcat | *Lynx rufus* |
| California myotis bat | *Myotis californicus* |
| Chuckwalla | *Sauromalus obesus* |
| Coachwhip | *Masticophis flaggellum* |
| Collared lizard | *Crotaphytus collaris* |
| Common king snake | *Lampropeltis getulus* |
| Coyote | *Canis latrans* |
| Desert bighorn sheep | *Ovis canadensis* |
| Desert cottontail | *Sylvilagus audubon* |
| Desert horned lizard | *Prynosoma platyrhinos* |
| Desert iguana | *Dipsosaurus dorsalis* |
| Desert kit fox | *Vulpes macrotis* |
| Gopher snake | *Pituophis melanoleucus* |
| Kangaroo rat | *Dipodomys species* |
| Leopard lizard | *Crotaphytus wislizenii* |
| Mexican freetail bat | *Tadarida brasilienes* |
| Mojave rattlesnake | *Crotalus scutulatus* |
| Pallid bat | *Antrozous pallidus* |
| Side-blotched lizard | *Uta stansburiana* |
| Sidewinder | *Crotalus cerastes* |
| Western whiptail | *Cnemidophorus tigris* |
| Whitetail antelope squirrel | *Ammospermophilus leucurus* |
| Woodrat (pack rat) | *Neotoma lepida* |
| Yucca night lizard | *Xantusia vigilis* |
| Zebra-tailed lizard | *Callisaurus draconoides* |

*Renegade Canyon*                                    — *Mark Pahut*

# GEOLOGY

The visitor to Indian Wells Valley cannot help noticing the abundance of both bare rock and deep sandy soil in the area. Bare rock makes up the magnificent skyline to the west as well as jagged ridges all around the valley. The deep sandy soils form the gently rolling, hummocky valley floor and at times create traps for the unwary motorist who drives off the hard roadway. How did this valley come about? Why are the rocks so many different shapes and colors? These are questions often asked, and perhaps this brief description of the geologic history of Indian Wells Valley, as it is now known, will help provide some answers.

The earth is about four and a half billion years old. We have no knowledge of the kinds of rocks that existed in the earliest times, although it is likely that the surface of the earth did not have a truly stable crust until approximately three and a half billion years ago.

The oldest rocks in the local area are found on the eastern end of the El Paso Mountains immediately south of Indian Wells Valley along U.S. 395. These rocks, once sandstones, siltstones, and limestones, are late Paleozoic in age (270 to 300 million years old). Their exact age is unknown because there are no fossils within them to assist in dating.

In the late Paleozoic era, this region was apparently under the ocean as part of the western margin of the North American continent. We can tell this from the types of rocks that were deposited during this period — limestones and shales, for the most part — which contain abundant marine fossils such as clams, coral, and tiny microfossils. Examples of such rocks can be found in scattered locations in the northern Argus Range, particularly in the Darwin area. Metamorphic rocks that were once probably Paleozoic sediments can also be seen just west of Inyokern as a prominent ridge rising slowly to the northwest, from next to the highway nearly to the peaks of the Sierra Nevada.

The next long unit of geologic time, the Mesozoic era, spans from 225 million years ago to about 70 million years ago. During this time the Indian Wells Valley area was no longer a quiet sea bottom. For a portion of the time, the land was above sea level and volcanos were active. Our area was in the very active western margin of a much larger land mass called Gondwanaland, which began breaking apart and forming the Atlantic Ocean during the Mesozoic era. The area looked much like an island arc, especially during the Cretaceous part of Mesozoic time, from 130 to 70 million years ago. Vast amounts of molten rock were emplaced at depths of 18 to 20 miles below the surface along what is now the entire Sierra Nevada range.

As these masses of molten rock pushed their way into the overlying sediments, they thoroughly metamorphosed them and caused them to recrystallize. Recrystallization changed the blue-gray limestones to white marble and converted the dull-colored shales and limey mud to brightly colored rocks called tactites and hornfels, composed of crystals of white wollastonite, green epidote, red-brown garnet, and milky-white quartz. One of the best places to see this type of rock is on the dump of the Hi Peak Mine, a few hundred yards southwest of the junction of U.S. 395 and California 14.

This metamorphosis also introduced tungsten in the form of the mineral scheelite. (The wartime need for this mineral brought prospectors to the valley; their small mines can be found throughout the area.) The cooling of the molten intrusive masses also caused the deposition of quartz-gold-copper-iron-sulfide veins throughout the surrounding hills. The best local examples of such veins can be seen at the Star of the West Mine in Wilson Canyon and at the head of Burro Canyon behind nearby Trona.

The same general type of activity resulted in the great gold-silver-tungsten ore deposits of Randsburg and Atolia to the south and the large, rich, lead-silver-zinc ore deposits of Darwin and Cerro Gordo to the north.

The cooling of these molten rocks or magma not only gave us ore deposits in the surrounding and overlying rocks, but also provided the many different masses of hard granitic rocks that make up much of our surrounding hills and mountains. "B" Mountain, east of the China Lake housing area, is a typical mass of granitic rocks, as are most of the higher, gray-colored peaks to the west.

The Cenozoic era, from 70 million years ago to the present, witnessed the final steps in the evolution of the Indian Wells Valley.

During the earliest part of the Cenozoic era, the valley was a fairly quiescent, shallow, nonmarine basin — the Goler Basin — which received sediments from nearby low hills that were ancestral to today's Sierra Nevada. The sparse remnants of that basin occur today in the El Paso Mountains and can be readily seen in the area of Last Chance Canyon.

Next came a period of broad uplift of the entire region, which was subjected to much erosion. Materials eroded from the uplifted ancestral Mojave Desert were carried toward the Pacific Ocean, where they were deposited in deep, narrow basins that today are rich in oil and gas. During this time also, the Sierra Nevada continued its uplift, shedding eroded material westward into a relatively deep basin known today as the San Joaquin Valley. This valley is full of oil and gas and hosts some of the most prolific producers in the United States.

At the end of the Oligocene epoch approximately 23 million years ago through the Miocene epoch, which ended approximately five million years ago, volcanism once again dominated the region. Very large stratovolcanos, some as large as Mount Saint Helens, dotted the landscape, spewing copious amounts of ash, pumice, and lava out onto the surface of the earth.

Features such as Pilot Knob and Eagle Crag south of Ridgecrest formed during this time, and debris from these volcanic centers came to rest in a shallow nonmarine basin and alluvial fan system, which has become known as the Ricardo formation. Rocks formed in this basin can best be seen in Red Rock Canyon State Park south of Inyokern. These rocks consist of sandstones, conglomerates, tuffs (rocks made from fragments of volcanic debris), and lava.

During this time, the area was also rocked by large earthquakes associated with movement on the Garlock Fault. This feature stretches more than 150 miles from the southern end of Death Valley on the east to the San Andreas Fault, where the Garlock Fault dead-ends near the community of Gorman. More than 37 miles of left-lateral offset are recorded on the fault, and the surface expression of the fault can readily be seen forming the northern boundary of the Fremont Valley approximately 15 miles south of Ridgecrest.

The Sierra Nevada continued to be uplifted in intermittent spurts during this time, the last such event occurring approximately two to three million years ago. This uplift coincided with large-scale crustal extension in the area of Indian Wells Valley and related extrusion of black basaltic rocks and pink rhyolites stretching along the northern margin of the valley into the Coso Mountains.

The rapidly forming basin, now the site of Indian Wells Valley, was filled with coarse-grained sediments shed eastward off the front of the ancestral Sierra Nevada or westward off the Argus Mountains. At the same time, large land mammals (camels, bison, sloths, etc.) roamed the area and fed off of fairly widespread vegetation in the form of plains grasses and shrubs. Fossil bones of these animals are still being found in the sediments of Indian Wells Valley and the surrounding areas.

About a million years ago, the action shifted to the Coso Mountains, where large, violent volcanic eruptions were occurring and forming perlite domes, which can be readily seen by looking eastward from U.S. 395 just north of Little Lake. These domes were surrounded by cinder cones and vents from which black and reddish-black basaltic rocks were spilled onto the surface. The best example of a cinder cone is known as Red Hill located immediately east of U.S. 395 two miles north of where the Little Lake Hotel once stood. Also in that area are abundant black basalts that flowed from vents in the southern end of the Coso Mountains.

*Red Hill from eastern side* — *Mark Pahuta*

The great glacial periods, in the late Cenozoic era, saw all of the valleys of this region filled with water to form a vast chain of lakes stretching from Lake Lahontan near Reno, Nevada, in the north to Searles Lake in the south.

For the last 25,000 years, the Recent epoch, the most significant changes in the landscape have been the result of climatic variations. Periods of high rainfall filled Indian Wells Valley with water to form a large lake (predecessor to the China Lake playa) and brought true forest plants down into our desert. Rainfall occurred most notably shortly prior to 10,000 years ago and again around 2,000 to 3,000 years ago.

Geologic processes continue today. Indian Wells Valley is still being filled by sand and gravel eroded from the surrounding hills. The depth of the valley fill as determined from geophysical techniques is nearly equivalent to the height of the Sierran Crest above the valley floor. The bedrock of Indian Wells Valley consists of Sierra-type granite and has a maximum depth of about 7,000 feet below the valley floor. The valley continues to be down-dropped in response to a regional northwest-directed extension of the earth's crust.

The Coso Range is the site of a large geothermal development project where steam and hot fluids heated by near-surface, hot volcanic rocks are used to turn turbines that power generators and make electricity. This electricity, enough to supply the needs of approximately a million people, is courtesy of continuing geologic evolution. Steam, hot water, and gasses emanate from hot springs and fumaroles in the Cosos.

The entire valley is considered seismically active, with more than 10,000 earthquakes of magnitude 1 or greater occurring over the last 15 years. These quakes are concentrated along two fault zones — the Little Lake Fault Zone, which traverses northwest across the valley from Ridgecrest to the present site of Little Lake, and the Airport Lake Fault Zone, which trends north-south along the eastern face of the Coso Mountains. As recently as 1995, the valley experienced a widely felt earthquake of magnitude 5.8 centered in the northwest portion of the basin.

Without doubt, erosion and deposition are the most obviously active geologic processes in the valley. Flash floods from thunderstorms carry boulders and mud into the valley, forming alluvial fans at the mouth of canyons, steadily wearing down the mountains, and filling the valley. Sometime in the not-too-distant geologic future, our valley will become a part of a vast flat plain at the foot of a subdued and rounded Sierra unless faulting continues to renew the surrounding mountains by dropping the valley relative to the hills.

Wind is also active, carrying dust and sand to the eastern edge of the valley, forming sandy hummocks and dunes, burying the base of the eastern hills, and carrying drifting sand on eastward into Searles Valley.

At Airport Lake and China Lake playas, dry lake beds found in Indian Wells Valley, giant desiccation cracks form as the filling of mud in the valley floor dries and shrinks. The same type of cracks can also be seen in Panamint and Searles Valleys to the east. All of the playas (which occasionally have water) are encrusted much of the time with white alkali salts composed of ordinary salt (sodium chloride) mixed with sulfates of sodium and calcium, borates, and carbonates. Many of these minerals are economically valuable and are mined on both a large scale (Searles Lake, for example) and a small scale.

Today, Indian Wells Valley remains a geologically dynamic place. Some say that the next great continental-scale fault, similar to the San Andreas, will traverse through the valley and follow the eastern face of the Sierra Nevada northward into Nevada.

Mother Nature has been kind enough to make the rocks easily visible to residents and casual visitors alike, and the opportunity to observe should not be lost. Please take the time to look carefully at the marvelous geologic wonders that surround us.

*Storm, Indian Wells Valley*                    *– Greg Turnbaug*

# CLIMATE

The planners of the Naval Ordnance Test Station had very good climatic reasons for selecting Indian Wells Valley. The predominance of fair weather with generally clear skies and generally light surface winds during all seasons has contributed to the successful operation of test ranges and, it is hoped, will now prove an enticement to retired Californians and new business ventures.

Located at the northern edge of the Mojave Desert at an average elevation of 2,500 feet, the valley has a climate that is beneficially modified by the mountains enclosing it. Most important of these mountains, of course, are the peaks of the Sierra Nevada on the west. Some of the local peaks exceed 8,000 feet above mean sea level.

The Argus Range to the east is dominated by Maturango Peak, which has an elevation of 8,500 feet. The El Paso Range to the south is somewhat lower, with a southwest-northeast orientation. To the north, the Coso Range features rhyolite domes, with 8,160-foot Coso Peak the range's highest point.

The mountains have a profound effect on the weather of the Indian Wells Valley, partly because airflow reaches the valley at low levels through four main mountain passes, and partly because the effects of the prevailing jet stream, which creates strong winds in the southern Mojave Desert, are tempered by the mountain walls.

Visibility is generally excellent, as much as 50 to 100 miles on a clear day in winter, with an average of 20 clear days each month. When low visibility occurs, it is generally caused by blowing sand or dust.

Valley residents have three major climate-related topics of conversation: wind, heat, and rain. When masses of white clouds can be seen boiling over the Sierra, residents brace for strong afternoon and evening winds. Trees, especially saplings, are bent by the prevailing winds and generally tilt eastward.

When the springtime winds blow fiercely, flying sand scrubs cars, housepaint, and the exposed skin of anyone who must be outdoors. Longtime residents remember "termination winds"— gales that blew across the loose sand of building sites in the early days and caused more than one Navy employee to terminate employment and move to calmer surroundings.

The most reliable indicator of strong northerly winds is blowing dust, a white haze sweeping southward from Owens Lake. If the dust blows only along the western side of the valley from the Little Lake gap past Inyokern, generally obscuring the Sierras, strong northerly winds will affect only that part of the valley. This situation gives rise to a familiar "valley eddy" condition, with east to southeast winds seldom exceeding 25 mph over all but the western side of the valley. If the haze obscures the Coso Range as well, strong northerly winds will sweep across the entire valley. Such winds are generally of brief duration, but have been known to persist for up to three days.

The Owens Lake dust causes two remarkable effects. Each microscopic particle carries a large electric charge capable of disrupting radio and telephone communication. The dust is also extremely hygroscopic, resulting in a radical lowering of the humidity.

The Sierra Wave effect is a special case caused by strong westerly surface winds. The mountains' barrier sets up standing waves in the atmosphere that extend to great heights. When descending air strikes the ground, very strong winds and dense dust storms result. In the meantime, under rising air, winds may be relatively light.

The most reliable indicator for such winds is lenticular clouds, smooth and lens-shaped, sometimes piled like

*Weather effects caused by updraft along the Sierra Nevada (looking south from the Bishop area)* — *Robert F. Symons*

pancakes at altitudes from 12,000 to 30,000 feet. These clouds, with their associated winds, pose significant danger to small planes.

Variations of temperature in this desert environment are extreme both on an annual and on a daily basis. Record maximum and minimum temperatures are 119° and 6°F. The daily variation in temperature may be as much as 30 to 50 degrees. Although night and morning minimum temperatures are cold in winter, comfortable temperature levels are reached by midday. Humidity is usually low in all seasons, typical of a desert climate. During summer months, houses usually remain comfortable with evaporative coolers.

The Indian Wells Valley lies in the rain shadow of the Sierra Nevada and has limited clouds and precipitation. Wide variations in the amount and location of precipitation can be expected. Prior to 1980, the average annual rainfall was about 2.5 inches; since that time it has been about 5.0 inches. The least amount of rain was in the 1989-90 rainfall year, when only 0.6 inch was recorded. The maximum was 10.91 inches in 1977-78. Most of the annual precipitation occurs during fall through spring months and is associated with weather fronts moving inland off the Pacific Ocean.

These same conditions cause our strongest winds during "dry" storms. During wet storms, winds are generally light. Increasing low clouds and light to moderate southeast to south winds occasionally indicate precipitation during fall through spring. A temperature near or below freezing may result in snow. The valley experiences a snowfall approximately once each year; appreciable snowfalls occur at intervals of three or four years. The heaviest recorded snowfall was about a foot in December 1984.

The most dramatic precipitation is in the form of thunderstorms or rare cloudbursts during the summer. The source of moisture is almost invariably the Gulf of Mexico, and sustained east to southeast winds aloft are required to produce the convective clouds and shower activity. Scattered showers and thunderstorms result from increasing cumulus clouds approaching from the east to southeast during afternoon and evening periods and persisting for several days. Such storms generally stay on the eastern slopes of the mountains, but occasionally pass over the valley.

Rainfall in showers is very spotty; only a trace was recorded at the weather station in June 1947, when a flash flood with hail of up to one inch in diameter passed over the China Lake housing area. Up to an inch of rain was recorded in the same housing area during a flash flood on July 30, 1965. That was exceeded on August 15, 1984, when nearly three inches of rain fell within a few hours; Navy laboratory facilities,

*Sunset over Owens Peak* — *Laura Austin*

businesses, and homes lying in the path of runoff from the nearby hills suffered major damage.

An excellent China Lake resource on the World Wide Web, *http://knidmidds.chinalake.navy.mil/clweather.asp*, offers thorough information on the latest weather conditions, as well as weather statistics extending back to 1945.

# ADDITIONAL SOURCES OF INFORMATION

## *Museums and Visitor Centers*

Air Force Flight Test Center Museum
95 ABW/MU, 405 S. Rosamond Blvd.
Edwards Air Force Base, CA  93524-8215
(661) 277-8050, *www.edwards.af.mil/museum/*


Boron Twenty Mule Team Museum
26962 Twenty Mule Team Rd.
Boron, CA  93516
(760) 762-5810, *www.rnrs.com/20MuleTeam/*

Death Valley National Park
Furnace Creek Visitor Center and Museum
Highway 190 at Furnace Creek
Death Valley, CA  93238
(760) 786-2331, *www.nps.gov/deva/pphtml/facilities.html*


Eastern California Museum
P.O. Box 177, 155 Grant Street
Independence CA  93526
(760) 878-0364, *www.caohwy.com/e/eastcamu.htm*


Eastern Sierra InterAgency Visitor Center
Intersection of Highways 395 and 136, P.O. Box R
Lone Pine, CA  93545-2017
(760) 876-6222, *www.r5.fs.fed.us/inyo/vvc/mtwhtny/*


Jawbone Station Visitor Information Center
2811 Jawbone Rd., Cantil, CA
P.O. Box 1161, Mojave, CA  93502-1161
(760) 373-1146, *www.jawbone.org, jawbone@ccis.com*


Kern River Valley Historical Society Museum
49 Big Blue Rd., P.O. Box 651
Kernville, CA  93238
(760) 376-6683, *www.kernvalley.com/news/museum.htm*

Laws Railroad Museum and Historic Park
operated by the Bishop Museum & Historical Society
P.O. Box 363
Bishop, CA  93515
(760) 873-5950, *www.thesierraweb.com/bishop/laws/*

Maturango Museum/Northern Mojave Visitor Center
100 E. Las Flores Ave.
Ridgecrest, CA  93555
(760) 375-6900, *www.Maturango.org, matmus1@ridgenet.net*

Old Guest House Museum
Searles Valley Historical Society
P.O. Box 630
Trona, CA  93592
(760) 372-4800, *www1.iwvisp.com/svhs*

Paiute-Shoshone Indian Cultural Center
2300 West Line Street
Bishop, CA  93514
(760) 873-4478

Randsburg Desert Museum
156 Butte Ave.
Randsburg, CA  93554
(760) 374-2359 (intermittent hours; call before visiting)

Red Rock Canyon Interpretive Association
P.O. Box 848
Ridgecrest, CA  93556
*www.redrockcanyonrrcia.bizland.com*

Ridgecrest Area Convention & Visitors Bureau
139 N. Balsam St.
Ridgecrest, CA  93555
1-800-847-4830, *(760) 375-8202, www.visitdeserts.com*

U.S. Bureau of Land Management
Ridgecrest Field Office
300 S. Richmond
Ridgecrest, CA  93555
(760) 384-5400, *www.ca.blm.gov/ridgecrest*

U.S. Naval Museum of Armament and Technology
P.O. Box 217
Ridgecrest, CA  93556-0217
(760) 939-3105, *www.chinalakemuseum.com, clmf@ridgenet.net*

# Chambers of Commerce

Death Valley Chamber of Commerce
118 Hwy 127, P.O. Box 157
Shoshone, CA  92384
(760) 852-4524, *deathvallych@earthlink.net*

Inyokern Chamber of Commerce
P.O. Box 232
Inyokern, CA  93527-0232

Ridgecrest Chamber of Commerce
128 East California Avenue, Suite B
Ridgecrest, CA  93555
(760) 375-8331, *www.ridgecrestchamber.com*

# Other Sources of Information

Death Valley Natural History Association
P.O. Box 188
Death Valley, CA  92328
(760) 852-4524

Historical Society of the Upper Mojave Desert
P.O. Box 2001
Ridgecrest, CA  93556
(760) 375-8456, *www.Maturango.org/Hist.html*

Kerncrest Audubon Society
P.O. Box 984
Ridgecrest, CA  93556
*www.ridgecrest.ca.us/~hallowel/kerncrest/*

# RECOMMENDED READING

Many of the reference materials in the list below were consulted in the preparation of this book. Others are sources of specific information on Indian Wells Valley and the surrounding area. Local libraries, outdoor supply stores, and museums carry selections of classics and newly published works.  Entries that are out of print are marked "(o.p.)."

## *General Information*

Broman, Mickey. *California Ghost Town Trails*. Revised by Russ Leadabrand. Pico Rivera, Calif., Gem Guides Book Co. 1985.

Clark, Lewis W. and Virginia D. *John Muir Trail Country*. San Luis Obispo, Calif., Western Trails Publications. 1977.

Farquhar, Francis P. *History of the Sierra Nevada*. Berkeley, Calif., University of California Press. 1966.

Irwin, Sue. *California's Eastern Sierra: a Visitor's Guide*. Los Olivos, Calif.,  Cachuma Press. 1991.

Smith, Genny, ed. *Deepest Valley: a Guide to Owens Valley, Its Roadsides and Mountain Trails*. Mammoth Lakes, Calif., Genny Smith Books. 1995.

Webster, Paul. *The Mighty Sierra, Portrait of a Mountain World*. Palo Alto, Calif., American West Publishing Co. 1972. (o.p.)

## *History*

American Association of University Women, Searles Lake Branch. *Searles Valley Story*. San Bernardino, Calif., Burck's Printing. 1975. (o.p.)

Austin, Mary. *Land of Little Rain*. Albuquerque, N.M., University of New Mexico Press. 1903, reprinted 1995. (various editions available.)

Babcock, Elizabeth. *Sidewinder. Invention and Early Years*. Ridgecrest, Calif., China Lake Museum Foundation. 1999.

Boyd, William Harland. *Kern County's Desert Country: An Historical Overview.* Lemoore, Calif., Kings River Press. 2000.

Boyd, W. Harland, John Ludeke, and Marjorie Rump. *Inside Historic Kern: Selections from the Kern County Historical Society's Quarterly, 1949 - 1981.* Bakersfield, Calif., Kern County Historical Society, Inc. 1982.

Chalfant, W. A. *Gold, Guns & Ghost Towns.* Stanford, Calif., Stanford University Press. 1947. (o.p.)

Chalfant, W. A. *The Story of Inyo.* Bishop, Calif., Community Printing and Publishing. 1980. (o.p.)

Christman, Albert B. *Sailors, Scientists, and Rockets: Origins of the Navy Rocket Program and of the Naval Ordnance Test Station, Inyokern.* Washington, D.C., U.S. Government Printing Office, Naval History Division. 1971.

Clark, Lew and Ginny. *High Mountains & Deep Valleys: the Gold Bonanza Days.* San Luis Obispo, Calif., Western Trails Publications. 1978, reprinted 1987.

Cleland, Robert Glass. *California In Our Time (1900-1940).* New York, N.Y., Knopf. 1.947. (o.p.)

Davis, Emma Lou, ed. *The Ancient Californians: Rancholabrean Hunters of the Mojave Lakes Country.* Los Angeles, Calif., Natural History Museum of Los Angeles County, Science Series 29. May 1, 1978.

Friends of the Eastern California Museum. *Mountains To Desert: Selected Inyo Readings.* Independence, Calif., Friends of the Eastern California Museum. 1988.

Gerrard-Gough, J. D., and Albert B. Christman. *The Grand Experiment at Inyokern: Narrative of the Naval Ordnance Test Station During the Second World War and the Immediate Postwar Years.* Washington, D.C., U.S. Government Printing Office, Naval History Division. 1978.

Grant, Campbell, James W. Baird, and J. Kenneth Pringle. *Rock Drawings of the Coso Range.* Ridgecrest, Calif., Maturango Press. 1997.

Harrington, Mark Raymond. *A Pinto Site at Little Lake, California.* Los Angeles, Calif., Southwest Museum. 1957. (Southwest Museum Papers, No. 17.)

Moore, Donald W., and Mark Pahuta. *Ridgecrest California: a Photographic Retrospective.* Ridgecrest, Calif., Maturango Museum. 1992.

Nadeau, Remi A. *The Water Seekers.* Santa Barbara, Calif., Crest Publishers, Inc. 1993.

Nakashima, Signe E. *The Cardinal Mine: A Ghost of the Past.* Bishop, Calif., Chalfont Press. 1995.

Peirson, Erma. *Kern's Desert.* Bakersfield, Calif., Kern County Historical Society. 1956. (o.p.)

Powers, Bob. *Desert Country.* Spokane, Wash., The Arthur H. Clark Co. 2002.

Powers, Bob. *High Country Communities.* Spokane, Wash., The Arthur H. Clark Co. 1999. (Powers has written a series of local histories, some of them out of print, but many of them available at the Maturango Museum.)

Pracchia, Lou, ed. *How It Was. Some Memories by Early Settlers of the Indian Wells Valley and Vicinity.* Ridgecrest, Calif., Historical Society of the Upper Mojave Desert. 1994.

Pracchia, Lou. *Indian Wells Valley Stage and Freight Stops 1874-1906.* Ridgecrest, Calif., Historical Society of the Upper Mojave Desert. 1994.

Starry, Roberta Martin. *Gold Gamble.* Ridgecrest, Calif., Maturango Press. 1974. (o.p.)

Thomann, Jane A. *The Zig-Zag Post Office and Its Neighbors.* Ridgecrest, Calif., Historical Society of the Upper Mojave Desert. 1996.

Weals, F. H. *Indian Wells Valley — How It Grew.* Ridgecrest, Calif., Historical Society of the Upper Mojave Desert. 2001.

Westrum, Ron. *Sidewinder. Creative Missile Development at China Lake, California.* Annapolis, Md., Naval Institute Press. 1999.

Whitley, David S. *Following the Shaman's Path: A Walking Guide to Little Petroglyph Canyon Coso Range, California*. Ridgecrest, Calif., Maturango Press. 1998.

Winslow, Sylvia. *Adventures With a Desert Bush Pilot*. Ridgecrest, Calif., Maturango Museum. 1984.

Wynn, Marcia Rittenhouse. *Desert Bonanza: Story of Early Randsburg Mojave Desert Mining Camp*. Culver City, Calif.,  M. W. Samelson. 1949. (o.p.)

Younkin, Elva, ed. *Coso Rock Art: A New Perspective*. Ridgecrest, Calif., Maturango Press. 1998.

## *Exploring*

American Automobile Association. *Southern California Desert Areas*. (Annual tour guide.)

Bryan, T. Scott, and Betty Tucker-Bryan. *The Explorer's Guide to Death Valley National Park*.  Niwot, Colo., University Press of Colorado. 1995.

Huegel, Tony. *California Desert Byways*.  Idaho Falls, Idaho, Post Company. 1995.

Jenkins, J. C., and Ruby Johnson. *Exploring the Southern Sierra: East Side*. Berkeley, Calif.,  Wilderness Press. 1992.

Jenkins, J. C., and Ruby Johnson. *Exploring the Southern Sierra: West Side*. Berkeley, Calif.,  Wilderness Press. 1995.

Lawson, Cliff. *A Traveler's Guide to Death Valley National Park*. Death Valley, Calif., Death Valley Natural History Association. 1996.

Leadabrand, Russ. *Exploring California Byways: from Kings Canyon to the Mexican Border*. Los Angeles, Calif.,  Ward Ritchie Press. 1967. (o.p.)

Leadabrand, Russ. *A Guidebook to the Mojave Desert of California*. Los Angeles, Calif., Ward Ritchie Press. 1966.  (o.p.)

Miller, Ron and Peggy. *Mines of the Mojave*. Glendale, Calif., La Siesta Press. 1976.

Munz, Philip A. *California Desert Wildflowers*. Berkeley, Calif., University of California Press. 1962.

Secor, R. J. *The High Sierra. Peaks, Passes, and Trails*. Seattle, Wash., The Mountaineers. 1992.

Starr, Walter A. *Guide to the John Muir Trail and the High Sierra Region*. San Francisco, Calif., Sierra Club. 1977. (o.p.)

Starry, Roberta Martin, and Suzanne Knudson. *Exploring the Ghost Town Desert: A Guide to the Rand Mining Area, its Natural and Historic Points of Interest*. Woodland Hills, Calif., Engler Publishing. 2000.

Stienstra, Tom. *California Camping. The Complete Guide to More Than 1,500 Campgrounds*. Emeryville, Calif., Avalon Travel Publishing. 2001.

Westbrook, Janet. "Day Adventures Within 3 Hours of Ridgecrest. Exploring the Northern Mojave Desert, Death Valley, Antelope Valley, Owens Valley, and the Southern Sierra." This informal publication of the Maturango Museum is updated periodically as needed.

Whitehill, Karen and Terry. *Best Short Hikes in California's Southern Sierra. A Guide to Day Hikes Near Campgrounds*. Seattle, Wash., The Mountaineers. 1991.

## *The Natural World*

Bryan, T. Scott, and Betty Tucker-Bryan. *The Explorer's Guide to Death Valley National Park*. Niwot, Colo., University Press of Colorado. 1995.

Cornett, James W. *Desert Volcanoes*. Palm Springs, Calif., Palm Springs Desert Musem. 2000.

Cunningham, Richard L. *50 Common Birds of the Southwest*. Tucson, Ariz., Southwest Parks and Monuments Association. 1990.

Dodge, Natt N. *Poisonous Dwellers of the Desert*. Globe, Ariz., Southwest Parks and Monuments Association. 1995.

Jaeger, Edmund C. *The California Deserts*. Stanford, Calif., Stanford University Press. 1965.

Jaeger, Edmund C. *Desert Wildflowers*. Stanford, Calif., Stanford University Press. 1964.

McCauley, Jane. *National Geographic Society Field Guide of Birds in North America*. Washington, D.C., National Geographic Society. 1993.

Peterson, Roger Tory. *Western Birds*. Boston, Mass., Houghton Mifflin Co. 1990.

Powell, Jerry A., and Charles L. Hogue. *California Insects*. Berkeley, Calif., University of California Press. 1979.

Robbins, Chandler S. *Birds of North America*. Racine, Wisc., Western Publishing Co., Inc. 1983.

Schoenherr, Allan. *A Natural History of California*. Berkeley, Calif., University of California Press. 1992.

Sharp, Robert P., and Allen F. Glazner. *Geology Underfoot in Death Valley and Owens Valley*. Missoula, Mont., Mountain Press Publishing. 1997.

Storer, Tracy D. and Robert L. Usinger. *Sierra Nevada Natural History*. Berkeley, Calif., University of California Press. 1963.

In addition to the above books, useful pamphlets, flyers, and checklists are available. For example, Maturango Museum checklists, all of which the museum staff keeps current, include "A Checklist of Plants of Short Canyon" and "A Checklist of Plants of Little Petroglyph Canyon," both by Mary Ann Henry; as well as "A Checklist of Birds of Indian Wells Valley" and "Valley Sightings. Bird Observations in the Indian Wells Valley," both by David Blue. Another checklist available at the museum is "A Birding Guide to the Indian Wells Valley" by the Kerncrest Audubon Society. Many useful guides prepared by the Bureau of Land Management are also available at the museum.

# GLOSSARY

Accipiter
A genus of medium-sized, short-winged, long-legged hawks with low darting flight.

Alluvial fan
A fan-shaped deposit of sediment formed when a mountain stream's slope is abruptly reduced at the mouth of a canyon.

Arthropod
A phylum of invertebrate animals that includes insects, spiders, and crustaceans with hard protective exoskeletons (skeletons on the outside of their bodies) and jointed legs.

Arrastre
Spanish for "mining mill," a circular rock-lined pit to hold ore, which was crushed by two weights suspended from a beam turned around and around, typically by a burro.

Atlatl
Aztec for "spear thrower," a throwing board and spear used before the advent of the bow and arrow.

Basal leaves
Leaves growing from the base of a plant's stem.

Belly flower
Nickname for the tiniest desert wildflowers.

Borax
A complex mineral rich in the element boron; directly deposited in arid regions from the evaporation of water in intermittent lakes called playas. Borax is used to solder metals and in the manufacture of glass enamel, artificial gems, soaps, and antiseptics.

Bract
A modified leaf, reduced in size, underlying a flower or a flower cluster.

| | |
|---|---|
| Bromine | A nonmetallic chemical element used in making dyes, in photography, and in antiknock motor fuel. |
| Calcareous tufa | A loose and porous deposit of carbonate of lime, formed by mineral or petrifying springs. Water charged with carbonic acid dissolves carbonate of lime out of the rocks, then as the carbonate bubbles to the surface, part of it is deposited again as an incrustation. |
| Caliche | A hard layer rich in calcium carbonate formed by evaporation on certain soils in arid regions. |
| Calyce | The calcareous skeletal surface of a coral polyp; commonly saucer- or cup-shaped. |
| Crustacean | Any of a group of arthropods (crabs and lobsters, for example) that have an exoskeleton, a pair of modified legs (such as pinchers), and two pairs of antennae. |
| Deposition | The act or process of depositing something, in this case rocks and soil. |
| Desiccation crack | A network of desiccation cracks often occurs on a desert surface as mud on the surface dries. These cracks, which break the surface into polygonal blocks, indicate a high clay content and are common on playa surfaces. See Mark Pahuta's photo on page 183 for a good illustration. |
| Down-drop | Lowering of the ground that occurs between earthquake faults. |
| Epidote | A yellowish-green mineral, complex calcium iron aluminum silicates, often deposited on metamorphic rocks. |

| | |
|---|---|
| Globose | Having the shape of a globe. |
| Horn silver | A common name for cerargyrite, a silver chloride, white to pale yellow or gray, darkening on exposure to the light. Called horn silver because it may be cut by a knife, like lead or horn. |
| Hygroscopic | Attracting or absorbing moisture from the air. |
| Hypothermia | A decrease in the core body temperature to a level at which normal functions of the mind and muscles are impaired; also known as altitude sickness. |
| Inverted siphon | A pipe whose height falls below the height of both of its ends, thus making possible the use of gravity flow across a topographic depression (such as Sand Canyon). |
| Ledge | Mining term for a lode or vein. |
| Lenticular cloud | A lens-shaped cloud that can result from strong airflow over the top of a mountain. These clouds can stack up like pancakes, often taking on saucer shapes. |
| Lithium | A soft silver-white metal used in thermonuclear explosives and in metallurgy. |
| Magma | A body of molten rock deep within the earth. |
| Metamorphic rock | Rock that has undergone a mineralogical, structural, or textural change in composition under pressure, heat, or chemical action. |
| Metate | Hollow in rock, used for seed grinding. |

| | |
|---|---|
| Numic | A group of related languages spoken throughout the Great Basin by Southern and Northern Paiute and Shoshone peoples. |
| Obsidian | A natural glass formed by volcanic heat and pressure. |
| Omnivore | One that feeds on both animal and vegetable substances. |
| Paleoindian | The period from about 30,000 years ago to about 10,000 years ago. |
| Palmate | Having lobes radiating from a common point; resembling a hand with the fingers spread. |
| Petroglyph | Figure or symbol pecked, scratched, carved into a rock surface, often by prehistoric peoples. |
| Pictograph | Design painted on a rock surface, often by prehistoric peoples. |
| Playa | A dry desert basin that often temporarily becomes a shallow lake after heavy rains. |
| Pluvial | Formed by the action of rain. |
| Potash | Potassium salts used in making fertilizers and soaps. |
| Raceme | A flower cluster in which the flowers grow along the stem on flower stalks of nearly equal lengths, with the oldest flowers toward the base of the cluster. |
| Raptor | A bird of prey. |
| Scheelite | An ore of tungsten. Found in contact metamorphic deposits and high-temperature ore veins associated with granitic rocks. |

Selenium — A nonmetallic element that chemically resembles sulfur.

Shaman — Native American medicine man.

Soda ash — Crude sodium bicarbonate.

Stratovolcanoes — Steep conical volcanoes built over tens of thousands of years by the eruption of both lava flows and pyroclastic materials (volcanic rock).

Trona — Sodium sesquicarbonate, a naturally occurring mineral . Used in manufacturing baking soda, glass, and other products.

Tungsten — A greyish-white lustrous metal with excellent corrosion resistance. Used in steel for high-speed tools, in electric contact points, and in lamp filaments.

Woolastonite — A calcium silicate oxide that occurs mainly as a contact metamorphic mineral in crystalline limestones. Used in the manufacture of tile.

# INDEX